To Kenny

to years in this
amazing industry

Great knowing you

BE LEGENDARY

From the Barbershop to the
Entertainment Industry

Live Your Dream.

Tracy Love

ISBN: 978-1-7360276-0-8

Dedication

This book is dedicated to my family – Sherah, Kaaria, Tory, Jaedyn, and Ryan for their ongoing love and support throughout my entire career. Everything I do, I do it for you. I love you guys forever.

Table of Contents

INTRODUCTION

Maybe you are new to this amazing industry as a barber or cosmetologist, maybe you have been in the profession for 10 years already, or maybe you are just thinking of entering the field. Whatever part of the journey you are on, my hope is this book will inspire you, give you some insight and answer a lot of your questions you may have throughout your creative career.

I have had a very successful career in this incredible business and I would love to share my experiences with you—the good and the bad, the successes and the failures. I have worked in three barbershops, a full-service hair salon, a major beauty chain, and six years in the hair show industry for Andis, one of the biggest clipper companies in the world. I have also worked for more than 10 years in the extraordinary business of the entertainment industry where I continue to work with major music artists that have believed in my talents and changed my life. I also work with Interscope and Sony Music Entertainment, where I continue to pick up newer artists as well.

My life is very unpredictable. I work long hours and the pressure can be overwhelming, but I wouldn't change it for the world. I am extremely proud of all of my accomplishments in the entertainment industry, I worked hard for it, but I also really love the barbershop; it is where I get all of my love for this profession, where my normalcy comes from, and where my passion lies. To me, the barbershop is where the culture lives. Its a place where the energy is endless and lives are changed everyday. I work in a great barbershop close to home with some amazing barbers that I have grown to be really good friends with. They are my shop family, full of great laughs, good times, lessons, and love. I also have a lot of great supportive clients, some of whom have been there with me from the beginning, that I really appreciate, and I am thankful for. A lot of good people come through there, and everyone is welcome. Although I'm really busy, always tired, and things can get super hectic, I love everything about the barbershop and this incredible profession, and I know that I am blessed to have such an amazing career.

Writing this book is a huge part of my life purpose, and I am excited to share it with someone who shares the same passion and strives toward the same goals. This book is intended for the barber or cosmetologist who is looking to have a successful career, and my goal is to give you the creative inspiration to follow your dreams. My hope is this book will inspire you to take pride in your work, push your limits, and help you become successful in the industry you have so much passion for.

There are a lot of inspiring messages, lessons and valuable information inside this book and I encourage you to read it all, but it is designed to help you wherever you are in your career, so if you come to a chapter that doesn't apply to you feel free to skip it, but if and when you need it, they are always there for you to come back to.

This is a very powerful profession and there are a lot of ways to become successful at it. It takes creativity, dedication, consistency, and most of all, passion. It ultimately changes who you are and even better, changes the people's lives you touch every day.

Although I have a license in Barbering and Cosmetology, my inspiration for writing this book is based on my love for barbering. I have 20 years of experience in the Hair Industry, and I hope that what I've learned along the way can help you. After all, in doing hair we all provide an amazing life-changing service with every client, and we all have bigger goals to attain that are intertwined with our strong desire for this awesome career.

So if the direction you are heading now is new to you or you feel like you need a creative push, you will find inspiration, guidance, and growth in this book to help you be legendary at whatever path you decide to take.

Remember: No matter what, you have the ability to do whatever it is you want in your life. The power is all yours. It's in your mindset. All you have to do is want it badly enough and have no doubt and no fear, and God and the Universe will put the people and circumstances in your life to make whatever it is you want to come true. Do not stop believing in yourself and what you are capable of!

SECTION ONE:

CREATIVITY
&
INSPIRATION

"

*The Highest Human Act
Is to Inspire.*

Chapter One

Inspiration

You can take many different routes in the hair industry. Whether you are a new barber or have many years invested. Whether you want to start a business, work in the entertainment industry, join the union for film and television, be a platform artist and travel to different hair shows, work for a specific product company, or even create one! Or maybe you simply want to just work in a barbershop and be the forever-lasting, everyone-knows barber. This is a career that is full of inspiration and opportunity. It all depends on you and finding what you like doing just as much as cutting hair. This book was designed to help you open your mind, line up your goals and get ready to turn them into something you can be proud of. Follow your curiosities...all of them and stick with the one you can't live without. This may take you some time and quite a bit of brainstorming, plus it can be a trial and error trying to figure it out, but this is all to be expected. Remember, overcoming obstacles is normal, it teaches you resilience and every lesson is valuable.

Like me, you may think you have an interest in something, but you discover halfway through it that you like it, but you don't necessarily have a passion for it, so you lose interest and move on. Or maybe you created something and it didn't get as much attention as you planned, so you lost the excitement and let it go. Don't be nervous or discouraged by this. It's okay to dabble in a couple of things that interest you. This may be the way you take your career to the next level.

For me, I started to create a travel bag to make my life easier when I'm on the move traveling or doing house calls. I shortly discovered that I didn't mind making one for myself, but I knew I didn't want to create a business out of it. People always said I should open up my own shop, but I knew the amount of work it takes to do that, and I didn't have the time. I am not saying never, but I know it is not for me at the moment. I also made an oil for hair and beards that I love using on my clients, and who knows, maybe I'll push for a product line soon, but none of these things excited me the way cutting hair did. I knew once I figured it out, it would be something that I would feel the passion for, and it would be something that I couldn't stop thinking about. After all, there's a bigger goal we all need to accomplish for ourselves to fulfill our ultimate purpose that can teach and inspire other people along the way. Besides, that is what makes the world go around from generation to generation. The things that I have accomplished in my career I really aspired to and worked hard to achieve. I have always been driven to achieve my goals no matter the obstacles. I was undeterred by the people who didn't believe in me or tried to stop me; they actually made me more focused. I know without a doubt, that if I had let them stop me, I would not be the person I am or be where I am today. And most likely I wouldn't have even written this book. I've learned to always bet on yourself and you will never lose. So, if you have a passion for something you want to do, or bigger goals you want to achieve, believe in yourself and don't let anyone distract or stop you; you can do it!

Throughout my career, it has taken me a long time to figure out what I wanted to do next. I have achieved much success and have accomplished many of my aspirations, but for some reason, I still felt unfulfilled. I knew there was still something that I wanted and needed to do. For me, I had to ask myself some questions and I had to seriously think about what it was that was missing in my life. I knew that once it hit me, I would be instantly inspired and I would know it immediately. It was like I could feel it right there, but I just couldn't put my finger on it. There were a lot of questions that I would often think about over and over again before I figured it out:

* What could I do that I would love doing as much as cutting hair?
* What else could I do that would make myself proud?
* What could I do to set myself apart from everyone else?
* What could I do to inspire other people?
* What could I do that I haven't done yet?

Questions like these would just flow in and out of my mind all the time, and more often than not, I could not answer them. I believe it's okay to not have every solution there when you need it; this is what makes us strive for our answers and grow with our intention. Plus, I believe timing is everything, and it is always perfect.

One day, March 31, 2019, to be exact, it finally came to me! Not too many people know the inspiration for this book came from the death of Nipsey Hussle, a modern-day philanthropist. I was so inspired by his tenacity and his mindset. He was such a genuine and respected person to so many people and was always giving back without seeking recognition for it. When he died, people of all classes, cultures, and ages came out and spoke about how he changed their lives. He had so many projects he was doing to encourage the youth and contributed to better his community. Everyone had their own story of what he did for them and why they loved him; he was such an inspiration to me. He made me realize my purpose wasn't fulfilled yet, and in my heart, I wanted to be the same way. I felt like there was something bigger than me that I needed to achieve to ultimately fulfill my purpose here on earth. And although he's gone way too soon, in some ways I feel his purpose in life was fulfilled as the inspiration he left behind will carry on forever through me and others he's touched; that will ultimately serve a greater purpose.

He said something that changed my life and motivated me to write this book:

"The highest human act is to inspire."

I saw this and I thought, He's right. How can I inspire people? What is it that I'm supposed to be doing here to ultimately fulfill my purpose? How can I leave a legacy? How can I reach my full potential? And it came to me—write a book! But honestly, people have told me before that I should write a book, and I always thought, what would I write? And where do I even start? But this time, it was like a light switch turned on, and as soon as I thought about it, all these ideas and thoughts just started flowing in my head. I couldn't stop them and I couldn't write them down fast enough. I was so excited; I felt it in my soul! I knew it instantly, and I couldn't believe that I finally figured it out. It took a lot of work, but Viola! You are now reading it! People ask me all the time how I made it to where I am and what better way to share my thoughts, experiences, and advice than to write a book. However, it wasn't easy. I didn't even know where to start other than to just start, and let me tell you, this was probably one of the hardest, yet most rewarding things I have ever done in my entire life.

I sincerely hope this book inspires you, enhances your creative purpose, and ultimately helps you reach your full potential.

"

We, as barbers and stylists not only contribute a lot to society with our talents, we are also part of a significant workforce.

Chapter Two

Why Cutting Hair Is So Special

Over the years, both cutting hair and styling have become a staple in communities all over the world! The barbershop in itself, since the beginning of time, was a staple for many neighborhoods all around the world and over time has created its own culture and has also cultivated its own sense of community. Interestingly, traditional barbers from when barbering first began were once considered surgeons and dentists as they did more than just haircutting and shaves. They actually performed small surgical procedures like pulling teeth, bloodletting, treating wounds, and smaller procedures like bathing and enemas. This is where the red and white colors of the barber pole initially came from. I'm not sure about you guys, but I am certainly glad those times have changed! I'm not sure I could have performed those procedures. Now, the barbershop is not only a place for men to get fresh, it is a therapeutic safe haven for them to come and share their life experiences.

Hairdressing, on the other hand, when it first began, was formed from barbering, then eventually as time went on, women began to branch off and have their own place to get their hair done and share their stories. Now, barbering is centered only around men's grooming.

In our modern day society, hairdressers and barbers are comprised of highly skilled women and men who are creative individuals that are very passionate about what they do, and express their talents by giving the trendiest haircuts and hairstyles they can.

The Hair Industry

Statistically, in recent years, beauty is a huge business. A very big business, as a matter of fact, according to the latest figures released by Groupon, from a study of 2,000 Americans on how much money they regularly spend on their appearance.

According to the study, they spend quite a bit. Women, of course, spend more than men: $3,756 a year (around $313 a month), for a lifetime cost of $225,360. And not too far behind, the men are also spending a fairly large amount of money to keep looking sharp as well. According to Groupon's figures, men on average spend $2,928 per year (about $244 a month). That comes out to $175,680 in a lifetime, 25 percent less than women, but still almost enough to buy a house!

People, in general, have become more aware of

their appearance and have made it a priority in their weekly budgets and daily regimen to get their hair cut, styled, or even just get a beard trim. Hairstyling products and hair tools (clippers, razors, blow-dryers, flatirons, etc.) have become a necessity in households for people to maintain looks in between services. Not only is it preferable for some guys to get their hair cut, beard trimmed, or just a shapeup once a week to stay looking fresh all the time, some are even obsessed with shapeups twice a week! And most women frequent the salon every two weeks for flatirons or blowouts, and for color once a month. It has also become necessary for some people to maintain a clean, well-kept look for their job, so their trips to the barbershop or salon are more frequent. This goes to show that appearances are important to people; therefore, so are you!

The fact that both men and women will spend hundreds of thousands of dollars on beauty over a lifetime proves that people are not only serious about how they look and present themselves, but they are also dedicated to feeling great.

In an article written by Danielle Pergament in Allure Magazine 2016, he states, "A survey was conducted in 2010, that 35 percent of people said they felt their appearance defined their identity. In 2015, that number jumped to 50 percent. So, it makes sense that almost two-thirds of people now said they work hard on their appearance." In 2019, I'm sure the numbers are a lot higher and increasing year to year. With social media being the forefront of our society nowadays, these statistics show the inevitability of how we have entered an ever-growing marketplace of consumers. Everybody wants to feel good about their appearance despite the cost and the amount of time they are in the salon or barbershop. From personal experience, on average, most men will visit the barbershop about every 2–4 weeks for a haircut and beard trim if necessary. Although I can say I have quite a few men that come in once a week for their weekly haircut. And don't be surprised if you have a client come in twice a week, once for just a line-up and the second time for a haircut. These men typically keep their hair shaved down to a zero (almost bald) and like their lineups fresh and clean. If they like the job you do, they will not have a problem paying you to save them time in the morning to keep them looking fresh. Needless to say, not only is choosing to cut hair special, but the beauty industry is at an all-time high and isn't going anywhere, anytime soon so you have definitely chosen the right profession.

People not only rely on just looking good to feel good, but they also get haircuts for many important reasons such as interviews, date nights, weekend outings with friends and family, or special occasions like holidays, birthdays, events, or special once-in-a-lifetime moments like weddings. A haircut can make a huge difference in people's lives; it makes a significant change in their confidence and can make a difference in whether or not they get that job they are seeking or that date they are hoping for. So, if you came into this industry to make people feel good, express your talents, and make money, you best believe you will! In this ever-changing, on-the-go world, you will constantly be working, changing lives, and making people feel their best. And that's pretty special!

The Barbershop and You

Not only is this a special job because you make a difference in people's lives, but this job also makes an even bigger impact on your life. It feels amazing when you can love doing something so much that you can feel the passion for it from within yourself. It becomes such a major part of your everyday life, you are constantly thinking about it, and you even catch yourself looking at people's haircuts and thinking "that's a great haircut!" Or "I know how I can make that a haircut better." You are constantly growing and focusing everyday on making yourself better. The opportunities for you in this industry are endless, and you should automatically feel the job security from the first day you begin because you know that people are always going to want a haircut, and you will always be in demand. We, as barbers and stylists, not only contribute a lot to society with our talents, we are also part of a significant workforce and should be considered essential to the community because we are not only capable of curating a substantial income, we do it with a touch of love.

Besides the service you provide, we all know that barbershops are more than just a place to come and get haircuts. It is a place to come and get your confidence back. A place to come and talk about all things from sports to personal issues. A place to relax after a long day of work. A place to come joke around, talk about endless issues, watch TV or sports events, and in some barbershops, enjoy a beer to start the weekend off. And when the service is great, it's also a place to bring your family and tell your friends about.

Bottom line, the barbershop is a special place for men to look forward to coming to. Most people will come back to you for years and years. You will witness your clients get married, start families, and cross major milestones in their lives. Over time you will cut generations of families, and sadly enough, you may even have some clients pass away. But through it all, you will meet some amazing people that do amazing things; some may even be able to help you out a time or two. Ultimately, clients are people who share their lives with you, and you may find yourself sharing your life with them as well. As you become close with them over the years, they will feel they can trust and confide in you and look to you for advice. You see, being a barber not only means you cut someone's hair, but you also become your client's confidant, therapist, and in most cases, friend.

"

Being a creative person is something to be proud of it is one of the best superpowers in the world, it's a gift and should be used to its fullest ability.

"

Chapter Three

Creative Power

This is a creative industry, and as you start your career, you will be looking for ways to grow, expand, and tap into your creativity. For that reason, I wanted to touch on your creative power and give you some tips on how to tap into it to make the most of your career.

Creative people make the world go around. Creative people bring peace and sanity to the world, believe it or not. It's quite interesting if you think about it. We cut and style hair, but it's actually a lot deeper than that; when people look good, they feel and perform at their best. We make the difference if they have the confidence to get the job they are striving for or that date they are seeking, which in turn could turn into a well-deserved job, wife, or husband.

Being a creative person is something to be proud of; it is one of the superpowers in the world, it is a gift and should be used to its fullest ability. After all, creative people made amusement parks, community parks, museums full of art, and pretty much all the recreational things we like to do on the weekends or on our days off that relax us and allow us to enjoy our free time. Even down to the sporting events we watch to entertain us. All of these types of physical and mental getaways are mandatory for us to balance our lives. Thank God for creativity and all the people who have a passion for it.

Because of the pursuit of balance and change, it isn't a surprise that creative people can get bored or an itch to do something else that stimulates their minds. It's almost expected, so if you have been doing hair for a while now and you're looking to do something else with your talents, do it! Your talents don't stop expanding just because you found what you are passionate about; instead, it sometimes opens the door for you to venture out and create something new for yourself. You are capable of doing anything you set your mind to, remember that! If you feel the need to create or feel something is missing in your life, maybe you should do something about it. Start within your current career and create a product or tool, freelance or become mobile, start a company, or create a brand of your own.

I say start thinking it, talk about it, feel your own creative power, empower your vision, and begin to manifest the next milestone in your life!

Create your Flow

As a creative, you have many opportunities and directions you can take in this industry. Just let your passion drive you. This process can seem tedious, repetitious, and times can seem challenging, but it is also a learning and rewarding experience. Keep a positive mindset, believe in yourself, don't stop, and trust me it will all be worth it. Remember to enjoy the process.

At the end of the day, it will make you treasure your craft, broaden your experience, and best of all, you will celebrate your progress, appreciate how far you have come, and be grateful for where you end up even more.

If you are having a hard time thinking of what's next, don't worry. We can tend to overthink—that's all a part of being someone who creates. We can have creative blocks, which is perfectly normal, so don't get frustrated; it will come to you. Blocks are a hindrance to creatives because it feels like our minds stop and we can't express ourselves. These blocks can be helped by incorporating positive thoughts and healthy habits, but most importantly, be patient and remember that timing is everything.

If you feel stuck, keep your mind open because it's important for creative people to stay motivated and inspired to keep the creative juices flowing. You want to create a momentum that will move you towards success. Don't get discouraged; stepping out of you comfort zone and taking a new direction, creating a brand, a new company, or the beginning of a new idea is not easy. However, you should be just as passionate as you are about barbering or being a hairstylist as you are about your new business venture. My advice is to follow your curiosities...all of them and then stick with the one you can't live without. Take your time during this process.

Creative Push

If you are feeling uninspired and like you can't come up with something that grabs and keeps your attention, the good thing is you can do some simple things if you feel you are at a standstill with your thoughts or motivation to be more creative. These things will help you think outside your box and set yourself up for success.

The first thing you can do to stimulate your creativity is to expand your horizons. Try traveling, reading books, attending things of interest such as going to museums, movies, or art exhibits. Explore all things of interest that ignite your creative energies and get your mind flowing. We as creatives are influenced by sights, sounds, and feelings. We take what sparks our fire and we bring it to life. There is no limit to a creative mind, so don't be afraid to expand and enhance it.

Another thing is to learn from the experts in your current field or your field of interest. Don't we as creatives often look to the best in our industry—our mentors—to learn new techniques to incorporate into our work and to come up with new ideas? Learning from other people can help motivate, educate, and give you an inspiring creative push in the right direction to help you transform and embody your vision. Remember, it doesn't matter if you are just starting or a seasoned pro, sometimes the best source of creative inspiration comes from others.

A really good creative rule is when a moment of

inspiration presents itself to you—get on it! At that moment, plan around your most demanding idea, the idea that you can't stop thinking about; write it down and keep track of any and all ideas during moments like these because creativity is a muscle that can be developed with constant exercise and healthy habits. It's something that can take time before anything really creates a spark. So be patient. Everyone and everything around you should inspire creativity; you just have to open up to it.

And don't forget to live in the moment; this will calm your mind, allowing you to find space to think clearly, tap into your natural intuition, and create a positive appreciative state that helps create an energy that spills into your ideas and goals.

> *"Imagination is the beginning of creation. You imagine what you desire, you will what you imagine, and at last, you create what you will"*

> - George Bernard Shaw.

Healthy Habits

Being healthy and forming healthy habits can really spark your creativity, relieve stress, and increases productivity. One of the most important things that should be at the top of your healthy habits list is to get up early in the morning and start creating! The most successful people you know and are inspired by are up at five in the morning getting things done. This is a time when your brain is more alert, so you can get a head start before everyone wakes up, it increases your productivity and allows you to work without interruptions. Along with waking up to get an early start, use these healthy habits to spark your own great ideas:

* Grab a coffee or your favorite beverage.
* Have a light, healthy breakfast to kick start your metabolism and fuel your body.
* Workout! Even just a light walk--getting some vitamin D from the sun boosts your mood and creative thinking.
* Meditate regularly to help yourself brainstorm, think, dream, and power down consistently to keep your powers of creativity strong.
* Unplug. Rest helps foster new creative connections.
* Keep a notebook to increase creativity as well. It helps to get into the habit of collecting and saving your creative ideas. It allows you to immediately write them down as they come to you, so you don't forget them, and it also frees up mental space and energy for other thoughts and tasks. So write it down and track your brainstorms. You will not only retain your ideas longer, but you will have more of them as well.
* These are just a few things that you can expand on and incorporate into your everyday life. Even if you just started with a few of these healthy habits, you will notice a big difference, starting with your thought process. I have noticed that if you are a creative person, it never just stops

after you have created something; you keep going because there's always more you want to do.

You are who you surround yourself with

I am surrounded by some of the most creative people and teams of people who make the magic happen. This inspires me to work hard and not give an excuse to say something can't be done. My experiences have taught me to remain focused and keep pushing forward no matter what. Because this is such a fast-paced industry and things are constantly changing, the last thing you want is to be caught standing still without a plan.

Getting to know many successful people through this business has allowed me to learn from some of their experiences as well. I hope to share as much as I can with you, so you can take it and apply it to your own life and career. When you learn through the experiences of others, it can save you a lot of time and heartache, and it gives you a much broader perspective. Yes, this industry can be tough, but it will make you a stronger person who works hard and appreciates even the smallest of things. This is important to recognize because, through all of my successes and that of the people around me, we know that the more you appreciate and are grateful for everything you have, the more you will be blessed with things to be grateful for.

Living in the moment is one of the most important things you can do without a doubt because along with a lot of other benefits, it helps relieve stress and overthinking. But, thinking creatively through inspiration helps to keep your mindset positive and puts you into a creative state where you are the most productive. Surrounding yourself or engaging with people you aspire to be like or that have the habits you are looking to acquire, changes everything. It is widely known to improve your perspective in your life as well as your personal and career successes. It will ultimately inspire you to expand your mind, step your game up, and help you reach your goals faster. These people give you energy and fuel your mindset into being great. Surrounding yourself with positive, successful people helps to consciously and subconsciously challenge us to be our best selves. You will find that they live in the moment, and more often than not, they practice healthy habits, are open-minded, optimistic, confident, encouraging, and are very mindful people.

I can speak from my own experience from being around some very successful, great minds that they always inspire me to practice gratitude, push myself, be open-minded, and help me include healthy habits and positive thoughts into my daily routine, so I can stay motivated and continue to grow and move to my next level. It's always about forward progress. I also find that reading books and expanding my knowledge is key to me having a better insight into my life, and it also expands my thoughts to help me think more creatively, ultimately helping me to become a better me. Hopefully, after you read this book, it makes you a better you.

Creativity takes time and energy but should be extraordinarily fun. The funny thing about creativity is that the more you do it, think it, write it, or use it, the more you have it. Taking advantage of other people in their creative works will not only keep your inspiration alive, but you will grow tremendously as an artist and person.

Remember, you can do anything you set your heart to, and no doubt you can do anything you put your mind to!

If you want to be a barber or stylist or are just starting your career or have been doing this for years, I guarantee at some point in your career you will want to do more. Maybe it's opening your own shop, working in the entertainment industry, starting a product line, creating a tool, starting your own brand, or possibly writing your own book! You are a creative! So, if you think you are done once you have discovered your passion for doing hair, this is just the beginning! Inspiration can take you a long way, so when you are ready to start expanding your talents, be excited and keep going!

"

*I suggest as you move throughout
your career you should always take
pride in your work and strive to
improve your skillset.*

"

Chapter Four

Being a Barber

Before we get started in navigating your career, I wanted to touch on the power of being a barber. It can be a superpower and can take you around the world if you are strong-minded and willing to work hard. This industry can feel overwhelming at times, but it can also be the most rewarding. Honestly, whether you are male or female, we are all going to undergo our ups and downs and times when we experience self-doubt; however, being a female in this industry does have its own difficulties, but nothing a little strength and persistence can't handle. All of my experiences have taught me something, and they have created the person I am today. No regrets here.

For me, cutting men's hair is something I have always been proud of. Although I had no choice but to get my Cosmetology license first and my Barber's license later in my career, barbering was always my passion and my first love, it was the driving force behind my entire career and from day one. The first time I picked up a pair of clippers it changed my life and throughout my career I always considered myself as a barber. However, I knew it was going to be a challenge because this is a male-dominated industry, and there were hardly any woman barbers around. I wanted to change this persona and work hard to become one of the best. I wanted to be in demand and respected for my talent. I knew this would be a challenge because I often thought that some men may not want a woman to cut their hair, and I knew I was going to come across that at some point. I would also think how could I compete with a guy that knows what a man would like, especially since I'm not one? But I never let it stop me. I figured a woman should know what a man should look like, and even though I never let it bother me, sometimes I had insecurities. However, I knew I wanted to be one of the top in my field and I was only getting better every day. Plus, I always took pride in my work and I was willing to work for my place in this industry.

For the first five years or so, I was always trying to prove myself and become better at my craft. I mostly had male clients, but I was open to doing women's hair too. It wasn't long before I realized that I wanted to learn everything and specialize in mastering haircutting—any texture, any length. I wanted to be able to take anyone who walked in the door, and honestly, this is the best thing I ever decided to do. Being able to only do certain textures or certain haircuts definitely limits you on the number of clients you can take. And telling someone you can't do what they are asking for can often leave you feeling unconfident and unprofessional. Unless you really don't like doing a service, I say challenge yourself and take advantage of the opportunity to make yourself better. You cannot become better without experience. It's imperative for your growth and success to take the time to learn a little bit of everything.

Don't limit yourself! Not only do you increase your professionalism, you also increase your revenue; trust me, it all will make sense in the end.

As you start to branch out and move throughout your career you will need to strive to improve your skills. I was always pushing to improve my services even if I was uncomfortable with the haircut or if the client was skeptical about coming to me. For me, the uncertainty of the client made me strive to perfect my craft, pay attention to detail, and try to give each client the haircut they asked for. Being a well-rounded, talented barber became an addictive challenge for me, and I realized it was special when I felt a more heightened sense of love for my talent every time I received a compliment. I always did my best to make it a point to never do a bad haircut because I didn't want anyone to say I did it. I suggest you push for your desired growth in your career, keep an open mind, take pride in your work and always push to improve yourself and your skillset.

After cutting hair for five years, I felt very confident in my skills, I was past the insecurity stage and I no longer felt I needed to prove myself. I had a healthy number of clients, and I was dedicated to my profession. Until one day I was working in a Full-Service Salon that was across the street from the Barbershop I worked at fresh out of school, and I was sitting at the front desk. This guy comes in and said he needed a haircut. I said, "I'm available I can take you!"

Hesitantly he asked, "There are no barbers here?"

I said, "I'm a barber," and he didn't say anything. I could tell he didn't want me to cut his hair, so I quickly said, "There's a barbershop across the street if you want to go over there." So he said okay and left. I felt a little discouraged; this was the first time in a long time, I experienced this and although I had a good reputation, none of that mattered if I wasn't even given a chance, but I told myself that this can be expected and I shook it off.

Three weeks later he came in again and said, "Are you available?" When he got in my chair, he apologized and went on to tell me that the barber across the street keeps canceling on him, and he likes to get his haircut once a week, so I went on to cut his hair. He became my client for years. I learned a valuable lesson from this, and I'm sure he did, too. You just need to work hard, and what will be for you, will always be for you no matter what. So, keep going and be consistent, believe in yourself, and most importantly don't take anything personal.

Later on in my career, I had an experience where one of my clients was shooting a music video, and I was there to groom him throughout. There was another artist who was in the video as well who I had just met. In the first scene of the video, they didn't need a haircut because they needed to be portraying themselves as if they knew each other from when they were broke and trying to start a company. Then in the second scene, they needed to show themselves starting the companies and becoming very successful. So to show continuity of them hustling in the beginning with no haircuts to becoming successful, I had to make sure they both looked clean-cut in the second scene. I could sense the other artist was nervous about me cutting his hair. He had curly hair with a taper and a scruffy beard, so he definitely needed it all to be cleaned up. He told me he never had a woman cut his hair, but needless to say, he was happy with it in the end and wanted me to give his manager my number. About a week later, his manager called me to do a house call for him. Ironically, as he began to be comfortable with me, he would say he was going to make me his personal barber because he liked getting his haircut by a woman because she knows how a man should look.

So being a female in a male dominated industry has definitely been a challenge from time to time and I feel as though I have heard and experienced it all. But at the end of the day, I appreciate it all. I think the biggest compliment I ever received was when I attended the grand opening of my friend's boutique called "The Wardrobe Department LA," which is a savvy clothing and lifestyle boutique filled with trendy unique pieces that are handpicked by my amazing friend. Anyhow, she is a stylist for the stars, and among all of her guests, Nas was there. He's a legend in Hip Hop, and I am a fan as well. He was standing near me, so I built up the nerve to say something to him. I said, "Hi, my name is Tracy, nice to meet you. I'm such a fan!"

He said, "I know who you are, nice to meet you!"

"You do?!"

"Yeah, you cut hair, right?"

"Yes, I do!"

"I know; it's an honor," he said and shook my hand!

I stood there for a minute stunned and thought, Wow! No one will ever believe this! I can't begin to tell you how this made me feel, but it made me realize that I was doing everything that I was supposed to be doing, and all of the hard times, doubts, successes, failures, accomplishments, and sacrifices were worth it.

Being a woman in this industry is a challenge and we can oftentimes go unnoticed, but this made me want to work harder and strive for bigger goals. No matter what, it's important to take the time to live in these moments; these are milestones, so they need to be recognized. They are most important because they validate the fact that you are making all the right decisions.

As a female barber, it is very important for you to also be cautious about your safety and surroundings. A lot of times you will be the only female in the room, so make sure you carry yourself professionally and you are aware of the company you keep. If you are a mobile (traveling) barber male or female, you will be spending a lot of time by yourself, especially if you are traveling between the shop, house calls, and gigs. This can be dangerous at times, and anything can happen, so make sure you take care of yourself and be aware of what is going on around you. I remember one night, close to Christmas, I was out late, working. By the time I got to my car, the parking attendant had left for the night. I got my keys from the front desk and proceeded to leave. I talked on the phone during my hour drive home, parked in my garage, and went to bed. I was awakened by my daughter asking me if I had someone in my truck or if I brought a friend home. I was exhausted and half asleep but quickly realized what she was asking. When I said no, she told me someone is in the back of your truck. I jumped up and ran outside as fast as I could. I was terrified, but I was more angry than I was scared, and before I knew it, I was out there in a rage! There stood this man I didn't know, holding my shears in his hand, as if they were a weapon! Without hesitating I yelled, "Where are my clippers!" I had no idea where he came from or how he got in my truck, and he had no idea where he was either. I was so mad, fear was not an option, I was about to seriously hurt this guy. I believe he was more scared of me than I was of him. He ultimately told me he thought it was his friend's vehicle, that he had been drinking too much, and he just wanted to sleep it off. I told him I didn't care who he was or where he was about to go, but he was going to get the hell out of there and never come back, or he wouldn't be leaving next time. He immediately dropped my shears and took off; I never saw him again. Luckily, this guy seemed harmless, but that could have been anyone in there with different intentions and the thought that he had access to my house and family throughout the night makes me still feel sick, but it quickly made me realize how blessed I am that we are always protected, and it definitely makes me more cautious when I'm out at night working. Remember, you have to always be careful and aware of who you are dealing with, and your surroundings at all times.

Yes, this job can be fun and rewarding, but being a barber of any gender that is in the shop full-time or on the go is not always easy. Most of the time you will feel challenged yet motivated to be your best and take this industry on head on, but along the way, there are also a lot of sacrifices that will be made. It can be bittersweet. You have to be confident about your work, be consistent in your talent, have the best intention, stand up for yourself, and make sure you are always on top of your game. Don't forget to always be aware and cautious of your surroundings whether you are traveling, doing house calls, or in the shop alone. Always trust your intuition.

SECTION TWO:

NAVIGATING YOUR CAREER

"

What I learned through following my passion is once you have figured out what you want to do, you must follow your heart.

This is where life changes and you evolve.

Chapter Five

What You Can Expect in School

Growing up I never knew what I wanted to do or what my passion was. I thought about different types of jobs, but none stuck with me. I had a regular job at a fast-food place where I was a manager barely making ends meet. I was always pretty dependable and a hard worker, but I had no idea what my long-term goal was. Then the day came when I picked up and used my first pair of clippers, and I knew instantly! I knew I wanted to make a change for myself, and I couldn't stop thinking about cutting hair. It was quickly becoming more and more apparent to me that this was what I wanted to do as my profession. At the time, I had a job offer at a competitive fast-food restaurant where I was offered a job as a district manager making 40,000 dollars a year, flying from location to location. I had the choice of taking the job or go to school to be a barber. Ultimately, I turned the job down and signed up for hair school the next week.

I had never thought of the hair profession before in my life. But I knew as soon as I picked up those clippers and had the opportunity to use them; I felt a feeling I had never felt before. It was instant fulfillment. Within a week my whole life changed and my hunger for this profession began!

At the time, there were only two barber schools in my area, and I wasn't sure if I wanted to attend the one closest to me because it was in a bad area and didn't have a very good reputation. The second one was pretty far, and I had to take public transportation. So, I thought about cosmetology school. While my heart was with barbering and I knew I didn't want to do women's hair, but I had to make a decision. So I thought about it, and I thought why not. I was eager to learn everything I could about hair, and I didn't want to put myself in a box. Besides, I figured I would learn to do everything from cutting short and long hair, color, makeup, and other services that would increase my revenue. My passion for hair had me wanting to be the best at it. No doubt in my mind I had a great love and focus for cutting men's hair, but I also didn't want to limit myself. I wanted to be able to take anyone and add on other services for my clients as well. So, I decided to get my cosmetology license and specialize in men's haircutting, later in my career I followed my true passion and got my barbers license as well. This was a major highlight in my career that I am proud of and it makes me feel complete and well accomplished. What I learned through following my passion is once you have figured out what you want to do, you must follow your heart. This is where life changes and you evolve. These passions can also lead to other aspirations you never knew you had. I believe we all have a purpose here on earth, and it's our responsibility to find what it is and live it to the best of our ability. This is how we all contribute to society, and ultimately, what makes the world go around. Although for some people finding a passion can be difficult, we all have one, and you will know instantly because there will always be a special emotion attached to it. Yes, I turned down traveling and making 40,000 dollars a year to follow my passion, but now I make more money and I fly all over the US doing what I love for clients I am proud to work for.

Barber or Cosmetologist?

Maybe you have it in your head exactly what you want to do. Maybe you love using clippers, and you know you want to cut men's hair, or you like to color, cut, and style long hair and you know doing women's hair is for you. Or maybe you haven't decided because you like to do both and you want to learn how to do a little of everything. If you haven't decided which one you are interested in completely yet, it's okay. You have several options, and we will talk about them all.

Now, due to the lack of schools and transportation, I decided to go to cosmetology school even though I knew it was in my heart to be a barber. I mean, after all, it is why I decided to do hair in the first place. I can't say that I wish I would have done things differently because my decision did end up ultimately being the best for me both then and now. It has allowed me to do all the things I have done in my career successfully. I can say that cosmetology school gave me a complete understanding and confidence as far as cutting long and short hair on men and women, which quickly made me realize that I wanted to specialize and master haircutting. Also, learning color and makeup just added on services for me, which now plays a major role in my Grooming career in the Entertainment Industry.

At the time, I didn't understand how all of these talents would play into my career today, but it definitely does; being a male groomer is a very rare commodity in the entertainment industry. A male groomer is a barber that does light makeup on men as well. This talent plays a significant role in everything I do today, it allows me to make more money per gig and get more jobs. Not to mention, I chose to further my experience and expand my abilities from after I got out of school until now, by taking classes such as Special FX, Airbrush, Color and other hands on classes whenever I could get the chance. My education along the way has really helped me with my confidence and made be better at my craft. Education has really helped me broaden my sense of understanding hair and technique when it comes to being creative on set or in moments of putting a look together. The fact that you are reading this book shows you want to be better and seeking inspiration, knowledge and skill is what will help you elevate. Your journey is totally up to you, doesn't matter if you choose to be a cosmo or a barber they both are extraordinary careers, and as long as you love it, you are making the right decision!

If you choose to go to a traditional barber or cosmetology school, both trades will dig deep into theory, client safety, rules and regulations, and sanitation, but they have two different curriculums. In barber school, you will focus primarily on male clientele, doing both hair and facial hair. You will learn how to properly cut, style, razor, and color. In comparison, a cosmetology program will have you work on both men and women, and you will provide a larger range of services that will include hair, nails, makeup, waxing, and skincare. I would suggest you go for the license where your passion lies, but if you want to master it all, why not go for both? To me it is a professional advantage and you feel unstoppable. Your talents are limitless and so are your opportunities. I personally feel if this is something you really want to do, go for it! And if you have a current license already, it is never too late no matter where you are in your career, to stack up on your credentials, and crossover to get your duel licenses in both Barbering and Cosmetology. If it seems like a major accomplishment, trust me it is!

Getting Your License
Hair school isn't what you would think it is. In the beginning, you are excited, and all you want to do is learn how to do hair. At this point, you have a

lot of desire and are waiting to become an amazing barber or stylist. Well, you will eventually learn to cut and style, but first, you will be in theory for a few months, which is where you are tested on understanding client safety and sanitation, chemicals and how to apply them, the anatomy and physiology of hair, scalp, and skin diseases plus more. Once you complete your theory hours, you will learn to perform haircuts and services such as color, perms, facials, makeup, nails, shaves, and more depending on your license. Each of these services will have to be repeated a specific number of times and get signed off by an instructor before you graduate. Overall, you will need to master tons of techniques and safety measures to pass the state test. Remember, school is setting you up to pass State Board, so it tends to focus more on customer safety, sanitation, and regulations than on styling and how good you can make someone look. So, while you are in school, don't get frustrated because you want to do more; just stick to the plan of gaining a lot of important knowledge about sanitation, hair health, and safety procedures to pass the State Board and get your license.

Later, after you pass your test and have your license, you will have plenty of time to take extra classes, attend hair shows, battles, and even find a great place to work where you can learn from co-workers. You will get most of your experience from the barbershop or salon. Don't get me wrong, you will have a lot of opportunity in school to learn how to cut, color, and style, but passing the State Board and getting your license is going to be your main focus. Don't worry or get discouraged; it will go by fast, and before you know it, you will be working full time on your own. We will discuss what to do once you have completed school later in the book.

Requirements

In California to get through barber school, you have to have a total of 1,500 hours. Usually that takes anywhere from nine months to a year, and cosmetology school is 1,600 hours and can take anywhere from nine months to one and a half years, depending on if you are full-or part time. You can also choose to do the apprentice program which is a training program that allows a trainee, called an apprentice, to earn a wage while studying to become a cosmetologist or a barber under the guidance and supervision of a Board of Barbering and Cosmetology licensee in a salon licensed by the Board. A contract called an indenture agreement is drawn up between the salon owner and the student apprentice. This is a full-time, two-year program. The apprentice must be employed full time (at least 32 hours a week) and receive supplemental instructions (RSI) in a classroom. After 3,200 salon hours and 220 hours in a classroom, the apprentice must apply for a professional license and pay the apprentice fee (All apprenticeship programs will charge a fee to join their program. You should contact multiple apprenticeship programs and inquire about their fees, what the fee includes, and where the RSI classes are located) and pass the license examination. There are quite a few other rules and regulations for the apprentice program. To find out more, go to www.barbercosmo.ca.gov or your state's barber/cosmetologist licensing bureau.

State Board

Although you have a lot to look forward to once you finish school, you have to first pass your State Board test and acquire your license. Once your hours are complete, you will submit a barber or cosmetology application for your date to go take your state test. It can take some time for your date to arrive, so in the meantime, study, study, study! As of 2019, in California, the fee is $125. I suggest you save yourself some time and apply online. Applications online are processed within three to seven business days. Processing time for submitting applications through the mail is three to six weeks. After you've applied and it's received, approximately two weeks later, you will receive the admission letter and a candidate handbook. The handbook will have your written examination date and time. Congratulations! So now on the day of your test, you will need your admission letter, the required supplies and equipment listed in the candidate information bulletin (current bulletin information will be on the www.barbercosmo.ca.gov website), a valid/current government-issued ID, and if you are a pre-applicant student, you should bring your proof of training (POT) in a sealed envelope from your school and a model or a mannequin head depending on the state you are in. If you are taking a model make sure they bring a valid ID or you will have to reschedule your test.

Regarding the test itself, it may vary in different states, but in California, the exam consists of two parts, a written and a practical. You will be scheduled to take both exams on the same day. Once you are scheduled, you do have the option of rescheduling the written examination to another day. However, the practical examination cannot be rescheduled. Information about this will be included with the admission letter that is sent to you once you have been scheduled for the examination. The written examination for cosmetologists has 100 test questions and you are allowed 120 minutes to complete it; the barber's written examination has 50 questions, and you are allowed 90 minutes to finish. Note: The written examinations for all license types may contain 10 additional questions. These questions are placed randomly throughout the examination and will not count toward your score.

As for the practical examinations, they vary in length. The cosmetologist's exam can last approximately four hours and the barbers for three hours. You will receive a 15-minute break during the barber and cosmetology practical exams.

Important: If you are more than five minutes late after the break, you will be denied re-entry into the test and will receive no score for the practical examination. You will also have to wait until the end of the exam to retrieve your belongings. So please be mindful of your time!

There are bulletins available on www. barbercosmo.ca.gov website that I recommend you check out before testing. These bulletins can be used to help you prepare for your examination. They provide you with the list of tasks that you will be graded on, the verbal instructions that will be given during the exam, and the required supplies/implements necessary for the exam. You must know how to perform these services safely and correctly and within the time allotted. If you happen to fail the examination, you will receive a score report that includes your score, a breakdown of content areas, and the number of correct answers needed to pass the examination. You will have to fill out an application for re-examination, which in California is $75. There is no limit to how many times you can retake a portion of the examination within one full year after you fail. But if you have not passed both portions within one year, you will be required to complete both the written and practical sections again. Don't get discouraged and don't worry; you will be more confident the second time around because you will know what to expect. Just focus; you can do it!

I know this is a lot of information for you to take in, but I hope it is helpful! I remember taking my Cosmetology State Board like it was yesterday, and yes, it was very stressful, but I didn't come that far to quit or fail! I for sure cried a few times that day, during lunch, while waiting for results and after they called my name for all the passing candidates. I also cried one more time on my way home. After it was all said and done, I was so proud of myself; it was like a weight was lifted off my shoulders. I couldn't wait to take the next step and start my new career. I was super excited! When I got my Barbers license it was only an additional 200 hours, it went pretty fast and by the time I went I was very confident, so the test wasn't as nerve wrecking, but the accomplishment definitely felt far greater. I felt instant gratification that I accomplished such a major milestone in my life. Barbering will always be my first love regardless and im proud to be in this industry. If your anything like me and you are in love with this profession, no matter how long it takes you, cross over and become double licensed!

Regardless, I know these test dates will probably be one of the longest days in your life, but you will feel the biggest relief when it is accomplished, no matter which license you to decide to obtain. So remember, make sure you study, get plenty of rest, and do not forget your ID; stay focused on the goal and motivated throughout, and have faith in yourself. This is just the beginning!

> *Always remember that no matter how long you have been this industry you want to make sure every move you make in your career is strategic to your success.*

Chapter Six

The Shop

Before we get started with looking for a shop for you to start your new profession in, or even if you have been in this industry for a while and you are looking for a new place to work, this information can help you with deciding on a new place to take your talents. Always remember that no matter how long you have been in this industry, you must realize that every move you make in your career is strategic to your success. You want to make sure there is a balance of talent and sociability along with a comfortable environment and stability. There are a lot of considerations to take when you move locations, not only for you but for your clients as well. This choice has to have them as a top priority because if they aren't comfortable, they may not be your client for long. The shop is a place that people have a personal relationship with, and they trust you not only with their hair but with your professional suggestions and decisions as well. Along with your decision to find a great location, always make sure it will be somewhere that allows you to strengthen your skills and motivates you to do more.

If you have just finished school, you should be proud of yourself. Congratulations! Now it is time for you to head out into the world on your own, an entrepreneur for the first time. Maybe you feel excited and confident. Maybe you have a plan all set up for once you've graduated and have a place to start your new career. But what if you don't? What if school was all you were focused on, and you haven't thought about what happens after? This can be a little intimidating since school was such a huge part of your life, and you became very accustomed to it. During school, having clientele was a given, and you didn't have to do anything but show up. Although you wanted to do a good job, you weren't expected to because you were a student, and you were still learning. The expectations were already set for you at school, and now you're on your own; this could push that intimidation bar for you a little higher. Now you have to find a place to work, and maybe you are having some doubts as to if you have gained enough knowledge to hold your ground in this highly demanding world of people that hold their looks and appearance to a very high standard. The first thing you need to know is: You've got this! Have faith in yourself, don't set limitations, keep the mentality of taking pride in your work with every single haircut for every client, and get ready to start living your purpose!

Creative Ability

Now, let's discuss an important reason to space out your career correctly and really pay attention to where you decide to work. These decisions matter and making each new move a success is a must. As you are choosing shops to work in, make these decisions based on becoming a better barber or stylist. Always push yourself and level up. Finding the right place has to include having the right environment and other talented barbers and stylists. It has to be a place you can learn from that allows you to grow. A place where everyone is welcome, and you get a variety of clientele. Finding a shop that can offer this is the perfect for you to become fluent in every texture, so take the opportunity if it also checks out to be a good place!

You want to make sure you will be able to grow more with each move you make, so I feel one of the most important tasks you could do in this industry, whether you're a barber or a hairstylist, is to learn how to cut different ethnicities. Familiarize yourself with different textures and styles. To do this you will need to put yourself in different environments throughout your cutting career and learn as much as you can to enhance your growth. You will also need to open your mind and take the challenge if you get presented with a new haircut, because being versatile with your skills will be your biggest asset and could catapult your career to multiple levels. I know this can be challenging and sometimes discouraging; it will take a lot of determination, courage, and confidence to keep taking clients you are not familiar with and doing haircuts you have never done. But I say educate yourself, watch other barbers or stylists, ask questions, take your time, think about your process, stay focused, and always look to improve and sharpen your techniques.

Learning different ethnicities is crucial to your revenue and, most of all, your confidence in cutting hair. To do so takes a great deal of time and experience but is worth every minute. Your goal should be, to be able to take any client who walks in the door. Or better yet, if your goal is to be in the entertainment industry, being a versatile barber or stylist is a major plus and will get you many jobs.

Here are just a few other reasons why throughout your career you will need to be versatile and take the time to learn to do different ethnicities.

1. For the Shop: It speaks volumes to be able to take anyone who walks in the door and wants a haircut. It shows that the establishment is professional and experienced. It allows you to potentially gain a new client just from being able to confidently say, "Yes I can take you. Have a seat!"

2. For You: It will allow your confidence level to be at its highest. It will allow you to move in a more consistent, organized manner which increases your speed between each client, enabling you to be more efficient with your haircuts, which equals more revenue. It will also

allow you to not be hesitant to try new styles on clients, allowing you to be more creative with the look your client is trying to achieve. Overall, it will give you a great understanding and visualization of haircutting and styling on anyone.

3. In the Industry: If you are looking to be in the entertainment industry, this talent can increase the number of jobs you can say yes to, thereby, increasing your revenue as well. Being versatile can open a lot of doors in the Entertainment and TV/Film Industry; you just have to be confident in yourself and your talent. We will talk more about the pressures of being on the grooming side of the entertainment business later in the book.

There are a lot of reasons to look for a diverse place to work in to expand your cutting techniques with various clients, but there are also some important questions you need to answer when considering the best location for you and your existing clients. Take the time to go through these below.

Finding a Shop

With these goals in mind, let's start the journey and look for your first shop to start your career! Go around to a couple of shops in your area and start talking to the owners. Get an idea of how their shop is run; take a look around at the environment and see if you can visualize yourself working there. There are a lot of questions you need to think through before you decide on a shop to work in. Aside from working someplace where you can gain knowledge and grow, you want to find a shop you and your clients will enjoy and have memorable experiences at. Let's take a look at some significant questions to consider when choosing a shop to work at:

Shop Business:
Services, Booth Rent or Commission and Barbershop or Full-Service?

Questions for consideration:

* How much are their services? (haircuts, shaves, color, etc.)
* Are they booth rent or commission?
* Will the owner offer you commission until you build your clientele?
* Is this a Barbershop or Full-Service Salon?

Services: These questions are probably going to be the most important questions for you as they are going to play a major role in figuring out if this establishment is for you or not. These questions go hand in hand, and depending on the state and area you live in, it will make a significant difference in what their rates are and what services they are offering. A lot of high-end salons in upper-class areas offering full services charge higher rates for their services. Therefore, if you chose to work at one of these shops you could make a lot of money, and I'm positive you would receive some good tips as well. This is a great opportunity for stylists and barbers who are fluent in every service and can offer quality work. Take note, the booth rent at these shops will also be very high, so if you choose a place like this, you would have to make sure you are ready to take on this responsibility. I recommend that if you have any doubts or concerns about covering the cost or the amount of responsibility you can handle, you can always offer to start as an assistant to the stylists or barbers and get used to the environment, clients, and services first. This is often the best route to go because you could learn a lot and apply those techniques to your catalog of skills when you decide to become a full-time barber/stylist there. This is also a smart way to go if you want to jump right into a high-end salon. I mean, yes, being an assistant may take some invested time, but your learning capabilities are endless. If I haven't learned anything else in the hair industry, it's that no matter what happens, where you go, or how many shops you decide to work in, nobody can take away anything you have learned along the way. And wherever you go, your knowledge will always go with you. This is where you have taken the time to invest in yourself.

Booth rent: Typically, if you are paying booth rent, you are your own business, so you will need to file for your business license down at your local city hall or online. It is not a long process, but you will be filling out a questionnaire with pertinent information associated with your new business. It will be a different price, depending on your city, but it shouldn't be too expensive. They typically go off of your projected annual income; for instance, if you are brand new and have no idea what you are going to make annually, you could keep your projection low, let's say $20,000, and your license fee will be based on that amount. In California I paid about $34 for the initial fee, so be prepared to answer that question. Along with completing the questionnaire, you will also need to have your barber or cosmetologist license available to verify and to fill out the required information. Also, think about what you will want your business to be called because that is what will be printed on your business license, business bank account, and business cards (yes, you will want to make those), and you will also use it on your taxes. In the next chapter, we will discuss taxes and other considerations for being self-employed.

Renting your booth means it's your space, so you will charge what you want for your services, although you may want to check on the rates in the shop you are thinking of working at and the going rates in the area so you can stay competitive. Also, when charging for services, make sure you are planning to stay consistent with your rates for every client, and when you are ready for a price increase give your customers a specific date well ahead of time when the price will change, so they are prepared. Renting your booth also requires you to be responsible for buying your own tools, products, and anything else you will need.

You will most likely have a key to the shop because you will be creating your own schedule. If you want to take a day or two off, you can, or if you want to take a vacation, you can. Sounds great, huh? Just remember that usually booth rent is due every week, the day is the owner's discretion, and whether or not you decide to take a day or week off, you still have to pay your rent on the day it is due.

But on the positive side, it is nice to have the freedom to make as much money as you want and have no one to answer to when it comes to your schedule or when you want or need to take a day off. The independence of it is priceless. In my area booth rent runs about $275 a week; that can range from $1,100–$1,375 a month. This adds up and does not include products, equipment, or anything else you may need, or any personal bills you may have. I suggest you have a steady clientele before you commit to booth rent. Most places that are booth rent only will give you a three-month grace period of either a discounted rate or will do commission with you, and hopefully, after the three months come around, you would have built up your clientele enough to afford your booth rent. I suggest if you take this route, plan on being there all day and every day that the facility is open to accommodate all the walk-ins and be available for the clients you do have.

Commission: Commission means the owner will take a certain percentage out of the money you make for the day. You will be able to keep your tips, of course, but the money you make on services will be split. The amount of commission depends on the shop owner and the going rate of the area. I've seen some do 60/40 (60 percent to you and 40 percent to the owner), which is quite high, but mostly I've seen 65/35. If you find somewhere that will do 70/30, that is ideal.

If you are on commission, you will most likely be on a schedule at the shop. Most owners like for you to be there all day every day, depending on their business hours, unless you have worked out a schedule with them. This is because the more you are there and able to take walk-ins, the more they are making money, and so are you. This will also allow you to build your clientele. The prices for the services the shop or salon offer are usually set by the owner, so before you decide to work there, make sure you agree with the prices and they are competitive for the area.

The shop owner should supply you with basic products like shampoo, Clippercide, Quats (disinfectant), hair products, and shaving cream, but with my experience, I suggest you may want to buy most of your products and supplies especially once you find ones you like. Hopefully, regardless if you are commission or booth rent, the owner provides the shop with a receptionist and towel service, so you have clean towels available when you need them. Of course, after this pandemic of 2020, towel service should be mandatory along with strict rules for sanitation for clients and staff, but that's just my opinion. Having a receptionist is up to the discretion of the owner, but it is very helpful and allows you to be able to focus on your clients and services without distractions. Receptionists also help keep the shop clean, sweep after each haircut, answer phones, and book appointments for you and other barbers when clients call. They will also be the first one to welcome a client when they walk in the door, can make small trips like lunch and errands, and even though you may have to give them a gratuity tip at the end of the day, it is worth it! Having a good receptionist makes it so convenient on busy days.

Being on commission, the owner typically will not give you a key to the shop, but I have seen some that do, but only after you have been there for some time and have shown signs that you are going to work there permanently. On commission, you can take days off and vacations, but these need to be discussed with the owner because if you're not there to take clients, they don't make any money and neither do you. Commission is a great way to start if you don't have any clientele because if the day/week is slow, you don't make any money, but you also don't owe booth rent at the end of a slow week, either.

Tip: If you don't have clientele, and the shop you want to work at offers both commission and booth rent, I recommend you start on commission. Once you have reached a consistent clientele, you will be making more money, so at that point, the percentage you will be paying the owner on your commission will outweigh the amount you would be paying for booth rent. That is when you would want to talk to the owner and switch to booth rent.

Once you understand the difference between booth rent and commission, it will help you make your decision about which shop or salon you want to work in and which one will better accommodate you. So whether you start with booth rent or commission, this should help you tremendously in considering if the shop is for you, so make sure you discuss it with the owner when you go to see the location.

Barbershop or Full-Service Salon: So, working at a full-service salon is exactly how it sounds –full service; they are salons that offer everything from men and women's haircare, skincare, to possibly nails as well. The goal of a full-service salon is to be a one-stop-shop, and it is ideal for an owner to have highly skilled, motivated, consistent, multi-talented people working there. This is not only beneficial for the owner, but it's also extremely beneficial for you because clients will be happy, and business will be thriving within the shop as well. It's also somewhere where the whole family can go and be serviced, so referrals to friends and family are almost guaranteed. If you can find a place like this where there are multi and diverse cultures and talents, you may have found the perfect place. Having a place that serves everybody means there are no limits to the amount of money you can make because everyone is welcome. It doesn't necessarily have to be in high-end areas either. I worked in a full-service Salon for about four years. I loved it there. There were so many different cultures and personalities.

The employees ranged from hairstylists, colorists, barbers, estheticians, massage therapists, and a nail tech. It was really fun and a great experience, everyone was nice, hardworking, and talented. We all got along, and we all specialized in different services and taught each other so much. We had so many different types of clients coming in there, and anytime they needed a different service, we would just recommend them to one of our co-workers. Since the client was so familiar with everyone, it was always very easy and convenient for them, and it kept all business in house. Full-Service salons are not just in wealthy areas; they are all over.

Typically, in a barbershop, the booth rent is lower than a full-service salon, and it generally only specializes in men's haircuts and shaves. These are very traditional shops that are a common place for men to come and get their weekly haircuts. Although, now that men are looking to be a little more pampered and groomed, they are open to going to a full-service salon, or there are now shops that not only specialize in men's haircare but they also offer a variety of services from haircuts, shaves, color, manicures, pedicures, and facials, just for men. If this is the case, then I would suspect that this would be a more exclusive place and prices for services will be higher, and more than likely, so will your booth rent. However, it may be just what you're looking for, you just have to really think about your goals and what type of environment you want to work in. Whatever you choose, make sure it's a challenge for you and you have room to grow.

If you are a barber just coming out of school and you are unsure, I recommend starting at a traditional barbershop to get your cutting techniques and skills to the level you want them to be. Get a feel for how the business is run, build some clientele, and when you feel you have reached your full potential and you're ready for change, do some research, plan your next move, and move on. Remember, if you do this the right way, growth will always be respected.

Still Undecided?

If you still haven't decided if you want to work at a barbershop or a full-service salon, let's talk a little bit more about it now because this is something to consider. Earlier I suggested that if you are a newly licensed barber, starting in a barbershop is the best route to go. Most barbers I knew went to a barbershop after they finished school; after all, that was the vision they had when they decided they wanted to cut hair. A lot of inspiration comes out of the barbershop, and most people that decide to become a barber, start there, which is not a bad idea because you can really get a true feel of how a barbershop operates and be inspired at the same time. You will also be introduced to hair shows and barber battles because when those type of events are going on; barbershops are the first to know. These events are always fun and super inspiring, you will learn a lot and have the opportunity to pick up new tools and products. We will discuss hair shows later in the book.

You will also have other barbers in the shop that you can learn great cutting techniques from to add to your own. You will also be able to see what products or tools they are using that you may like, ask all the questions you want, and I'm sure at some point that you will need to work on your tools and adjust your clippers, such as zero gapping, and you can get help on learning those techniques as well. There are so many things to anticipate and be excited about when you work in a barbershop for the first time.

When I first got out of school, I worked at a barbershop. I loved working there and I learned a lot. I remember when I wasn't' able to do the greatest fade, and the barbers would make fun of me after the client left. And even though I laughed it off, it really made me a better barber. It made me pay attention to detail and use my mirror to see where my weight lines were in my haircuts so I could make my fades better. I remember being excited to learn different techniques and incorporate them into my cutting style. Over the four years I worked there, I learned so much and made some great friends. I talk more about the type of barbershops I worked in and why later on in the book. But overall, being in a barbershop straight out of school can bring many great experiences and a lot of fun memories. And, if you find a busy one, you can look forward to a lot of new clients looking for a barber they can not only talk to, laugh with, and confide in every two weeks, but also trust with their appearance. Yes, that could be you!

Now, there are benefits of working in a full-service salon as well. Because they serve both men and women, this is ideal for a cosmologist, but if you are a barber and you are interested in cosmetology too, you could look into working at a full-service salon and look forward to learning different services such as cutting, styling long hair, coloring, and more. There will be a lot of stylists there doing color, so you could watch, ask questions, and possibly be able to work with color on some of your clients while not being intimidated because you have a lot of great help right there. Sometimes in a barbershop, men won't ask for color unless they are concerned with gray hair coming in, and even then, sometimes they're a little hesitant or won't even ask at all. But if they were in a full-service salon, they will see color being done often and are more apt to inquire—if not just to cover their gray, then to possibly change their natural color to something trendy.

I recommend taking the time to take some hands-on classes outside of your shop, tons of classes are put on by your favorite companies, from clipper cutting, haircutting and styles, coloring, braiding, hair extensions, building your business, and more. There are also tons of videos online to grab ideas from or learn from co-workers and get experience in all types of services because you never know when you will be asked if you can do a service, and you don't want to have to say no from lack of experience. The more you know, the more money you can make, it's that simple. I also worked in a full-service salon for three years, and I learned a lot while I was there, and I got full experience in coloring and styling long and short hair. I am certainly glad I did it. If you plan on taking your talents to the entertainment industry, you will want to be well rounded in all aspects of hair. We will discuss the entertainment industry later on in the book as well.

Shop Scene:
Location, Success, Days and Hours

Questions for consideration:

Is the location close to home?

* Is the location in a great area for customers to walk in?
* Is the shop busy at the moment?
* What are the days and hours of operation?

Location and Success: One thing you definitely want to consider is commute time. Is the shop busy enough for you to make the commute worth it? If the shop is reputable, in a busy area, and close to home, perfect! If not, take a look around while you're in the shop and see if it is busy with clients or if the barbers are just sitting around. Not to say the shop will be busy all the time, but before you ultimately decide to work there, you should visit a couple of times possibly on a Monday or Tuesday, and then again on a busy Friday.

Regardless, depending on the day of the week, clients should be coming in and out or calling to schedule appointments. You want to make sure of this because building clientele for yourself is important, and it may also take some time.

Ultimately, this will let you know if making this commitment is worth it, and it will make a huge difference in your decision to work there. Ideally, you want your workplace to be close to you and as accessible as possible, but it is also important for the shop to be in a great location to ensure a high walk-in ratio. As I said, this will not only help you build clientele but will also put consistent money in your pocket.

Days and hours of operation: You will need to take into account the days and hours of operation. Most shops, if you are commission, want you to be there from open to close all the time. Like I said earlier, if you are not there, the owner doesn't make any money in case of a walk-in, and neither do you, but also it will be hard for you to build a steady clientele if you are not there. So for the first year plan on being there all the time. Also, if you are unavailable during any days or times, you need to discuss that with the owner before you start. Back in the day, shops were closed Sunday and Monday because these were the days that hair shows and classes took place for furthering education, but nowadays, operating times and days open are at the owner's discretion. Now, some are only closed on Sunday, but I have found some are open seven days a week. Regardless of the days and times the shop is open, if you can be in the shop constantly, do it so you can build your clientele and become established.

Shop Environment:
First impression, Barber/Stylists friendly, Customer Service, Longevity and Quality Work.

Questions for consideration:

* What first impression did you get when you walked in?
* Do the other barbers and stylists seem friendly?
* Do they have good customer service?
* Are there barbers or stylists that have been there for a long time?
* Does the shop give quality work?

First impression: So, when you go into a shop or salon for the first time looking to work there, you want to pay attention to the energy and vibe of the shop as soon as you walk in. Pay attention to how it makes you feel. Does someone greet you as soon as you walk in? Is it clean? Is there a TV or music playing in the background, setting the mood? It's important to notice all of these things. It should have some liveliness, a feel-good flow, great conversation, and a welcoming feeling. This will be the same experience your clients or a new client will have when they walk in, too. You only get one chance at this, so don't forget to take notice.

Barbers/Stylists friendly: Observe if the barbers or stylists seem friendly or not when you inquire about working there. Were they willing to assist you? Are they having conversations with their clients? Do the clients look happy? Remember, you will be working side by side with these same people, and it can be hard if you have a co-worker that isn't so nice and doesn't have a good attitude towards others. This is important especially since you will be spending a significant amount of time together in a rather small space. If they are rude, these are not the type of co-workers you can look to for help, guidance, and inspiration when you need it. As I mentioned before, the first impression is important and speaks volumes about a place.

Customer Service: Additionally, you want to make sure that the clients feel they are getting good service. Customer service and a good haircut go hand in hand. If someone gets a good haircut but bad vibes every time they go into a shop, they may not come back at some point. And you can forget them suggesting to someone else to go there, and vice versa. There are quite a few competitive shops and a lot of great barbers and stylists out there ready to take on a new client. Making sure your clients are comfortable and enjoy the barbershop experience will keep them coming back. Even if you might not have given them the exact haircut they wanted but the environment was pleasant, they will most likely still return to give you another try. When someone goes somewhere for the first time and has a great experience, they may tell a few people that day, but if someone has a bad experience, they will tell everybody they encounter how bad their experience was. Do not be that bad experience.

I have known other barbers and stylists who didn't really care if the client was satisfied or if they would become a returning customer. I have also heard people complain about bad haircuts or that their barber was always canceling or wasn't showing up for appointments. Some would hurry up to get the client out and skip on certain things, like not cutting the hair on someone's neck once the cape was undone. These types of bad habits will never keep a client coming back no matter how skilled you are. I learned that reliability and attention to detail are essential. Every customer not only wants your complete attention while they are with you, but they also always want a good haircut

Longevity: When you have your first conversation with the manager and you are asking them your list of questions, inquire if there are any barbers or stylists that have been there for a long time. This not only shows you longevity in the shop but it says a lot about the owner and their business tactics. Plus, there's nothing like having an experienced, friendly co-worker that is willing to share their knowledge with you and show you a trick or two.

Ask yourself if this is a place you can grow. Remember, people can take everything from you, but they can't take away your experience and what you have acquired through the years. What you learn along the way is what will make you an amazing barber or stylist. So having people around that are grounded and have a good business ethic will help you in creating good customer service and longevity for yourself as well. Experience will make you irreplaceable.

Quality Work: So, when you walk into a shop for the first time, take notice if the barbers or stylists are doing a good job on their clients. You might want to stay around to see a few leave. It's important to notice this for a couple of reasons. One, if the client is leaving with a bad haircut or color/style, people that are outside don't know it wasn't you that did the service; they don't know who did it, so they will attribute it to the entire shop, and most likely won't go there for services if they don't like what they see. Whatever comes out of your shop in terms of quality of the work and customer service makes a difference in whether clients will come back or refer other clients, so this affects everyone in the shop, including you. I have had clients tell me that when they are going somewhere new for a haircut, they will sit outside and watch customers come out before they decide if they want to go there. This is a quality your new shop must have, or it may be a deal-breaker for you. Plus, if you see the great work coming out of there, you know that you will be able to join a talented team that you can watch, learn, ask questions, and build with.

Shop Expectations:
Cleanliness/Regulations and Staying Prepared

Questions to consider:

* Is the Shop Clean?
* Are you prepared for State Board?

Every shop has expectations it must meet based on the State Board requirements. So as you check out the shop, you will want to make sure, it is clean and meets the rules and regulations. You may not know what all of these regulations are, but if the shop is clean and licenses are noticeable, these are good signs that the shop is up to standards.

Cleanliness/Regulations: Now, ask yourself if this a place you would come to get your hair done? Is the shop clean and well maintained? Does this shop have a receptionist to help maintain the shop's cleanliness; if not, do they have a cleaning crew that comes in on the weekends to clean the shop so it is ready to go for the next week? There's a lot involved with finding the perfect place, but along with great customer service, you want to make sure the shop is up to standards. It may seem like a lot to go through but if you nail everything you are looking for in a shop, you will have fewer problems later, and you can just enjoy getting paid for what you love to do.

Cleanliness of the shop is high on the list of priorities. If the State Board decides to pay an unexpected visit, you don't want them to find anything wrong and start issuing fines, because if they find a lot of problems, not only will this be expensive, they will come back often to make sure the shop is up to standards. For more information on the type of fines and the amounts, they are required to be posted on the wall at the shop or you can look them up on The Board of Barbering and Cosmetology website under laws and regulations for your state.

Staying Prepared: There is a lot to know, the standards are high, and you will have to keep up with all the regulations, especially if you are a shop owner. But if you are a barber or stylist, only a portion of these apply to you, so if you just keep up with the basics of sanitation regularly, you will be fine. Generally, the owner will be good at staying up on these codes and standards because the fines are steep. However, the owner may be on you to keep up with your sanitation requirements as well because if State Board walks in and fines you, whatever you are fined for, the owner will be fined as well. It is a double fine, so it is very important to keep up with keeping your area clean, following sanitation rules, and making sure your station and things are labeled correctly. Fines start at one hundred dollars. So, when you're checking out the shop, make sure it appears to value these codes. You can tell quickly by looking around and noticing if you see any labels marked soiled or clean, if the shop's business license is hanging in a noticeable area, and if the barbers or stylists have their licenses hanging in clear view as well. All of these should be pretty noticeable.

When you start working, follow these key tips to make sure you are prepared:

* Have your license/business license visibly displayed at your station.
* Label all of your belongings appropriately (soiled, clean, water, etc.).
* Have clean Barbicide (disinfectant solution) in an appropriate jar for your soiled implements (change frequently).
* Keep your area clean (no Sanex strips on the floor; you will be fined).
* Have a proper disposal container (make sure it is labeled) for your razors and make sure none are exposed; this is a big fine!

I recommend you make these tips second nature so you can keep up with it easily. Your school will go over this while you are there. I learned quickly how important it is to know your sanitation rules on implements and why to follow State Board rules to the best of your ability.

The first barbershop I worked at, the State Board paid us an unexpected visit. I was fairly new, and the owner had removed the business license that day to go take care of some business. Shortly after State Board came in, he walked directly to me and asked me what procedure I used to sanitize my implements and tools, so I told him exactly what I learned in school; he took note and walked away. Then he recognized that the business license for the shop wasn't posted and gave me a $1,500 fine for it because he said it appeared I was working in an unlicensed establishment. I was also the only one fined, so when I asked why, he said it was because I was in the first chair. I tried to explain why the license wasn't there, and he said to have the owner handle it. So, I called State Board the next day and they talked to the owner. I had to fax a copy of the business license, but luckily, they approved it and dismissed the fine. Whew! State Board does not have the friendliest staff and they can be very intimidating and harsh, so make sure you cover your end and make sure you know and follow all standards and procedures.

Shop Standards:
Lighting, Station Standards, Fresh Towels and Reviews

Questions for your consideration:

* Is the lighting good?
* Does your station meet standards with enough space and mats to stand on while working?
* Do they have a towel service?
* What is the shop's Yelp reviews and ratings?

Good lighting: An important thing to look for in your potential new workplace is if the lighting is adequate. Your shop needs to be well lit. Appropriate lighting is very, very important. This is going to help your haircuts look their best. The wrong lightbulbs can make a huge difference in the time it takes for you to finish your haircuts efficiently and how good your haircuts end up as well. When the lighting is correct, you will be able to see where the weight is in your fades and avoid seeing shadows. With inaccurate lighting, even if you use your mirror to see where weight lines are in your haircuts, you will have dark shadowed areas, making it very hard to complete. The worst part of not being able to see accurately is you will be straining your eyes, moving slowly to avoid mistakes, and ultimately taking longer for you to finish the haircut. Also, when you are finished and they get up, you will observe the haircut and notice the areas that need to be touched up again, but at this point, it's too late. Typically, shops will have light panels on the ceiling and a light over each station. Ultimately, you will need an LED lightbulb; these tend to give the best accurate light we need.

Pro Tip: I suggest you practice not looking in the mirror so you're not relying on it and are prepared when you don't have it. Learn to see your weight lines without one. Because if you decide to do house calls or work in entertainment, you will not always have accurate lighting or a mirror to depend on. Also, if you are on the go and cutting in inadequate light and you are having a hard time seeing, use a headlight. This is a tool I rely on when I'm on the move and I have minimal light and no mirror. It takes practice to learn how to not use your mirror, but you'll get good at, so start now.

Station Standards: Something else to consider is if the stations have enough space for you and your equipment. There are a lot of different types of stations that the owner could choose from. Some shops have smaller stations so they can have more barbers or stylists; thus, the amount of space you might end up having may be tight. So, if you notice that there are a lot of stations in a small shop, you may want to make sure you will have enough space and ask yourself how comfortable you and your clients will be. You can always purchase a roll-a-bout to use for additional space, but you will need room either next to or underneath your station to store it. So, make sure that there is space for products, tools, blow dryer, plus any extra equipment. Hopefully, the owner has an extra storage unit for you so you can have an additional area to store things you typically don't use all the time; plus this will also give you some extra space for your personal belongings.

Another very important aspect of your potential workplace is making sure you have mats around your chair to support your legs and feet while working. This may not sound important, but after a long day it is because remember, you will be working extended hours and standing for most of the day, so these mats will help your legs, feet, and back from aching. If you don't have a mat at your station, and you're on commission you can request that the owner supply you with one; however, if you are booth rent, you may have to purchase your own. But the upside of getting your own is you can purchase one you like, and if you ever leave, you can take your property with you.

Fresh Towels: Then, of course, you are expected to

keep your area and tools clean. Having a sanitized area, clean tools, implements, and towels are going to be an ongoing priority to ensure your client's health and everyone's safety. Especially after the COVID-19 pandemic, things may never be the same. If you can find a shop that offers towel service, that would be ideal. Not all of them do as it is more of a privilege than a necessity. It used to be that a lot of shops preferred to have a washer and dryer on the premises to save some money, and I'm not just talking about mom and pop shops. I've seen major franchises have them as well. So, there it would be part of the receptionist's job to fold and keep them stocked. It is nice to find an owner who cares enough to have fresh, clean towels every week delivered from a professional towel company; however, it may become a regulation soon for all owners to supply fresh towels.

Yelp Reviews: Last but not least, go on Yelp to help you find a few places to visit. Look at the ratings and read the reviews to help you find out what the good aspects of the shop are and what problems they may be having. You can definitely see who has the best customer service and the worst, who does great work and who doesn't, and you may also be able to find out if people have complaints about the owner or if they are great and amazing at solving issues. Keep in mind, potential clients use this tool for the same reasons, so you want to make sure you bring your A-game all the time when you are at work.

Hopefully, this helps you pick the perfect place. I have seen quite a few barbershops where rules and regulations are nonexistent, and there is little respect for the business and clients, which is very unprofessional. The owners of these shops ultimately lack good leadership or communication skills. So these are the types of shops you want to avoid. They should have good systems in place for scheduling, receiving payment, and as well for the barbers and stylists to pay their commission or booth rent. There has to be a lot of respect between the employees and the owner. The shop, as a whole, needs to understand proper customer service and want to be successful for a shop to flow, have happy employees, and in turn, have happy returning customers. So at the end of the day, not only will you be spending a lot of time in your future workplace with the owner and in the company of your co-workers, so will your clients!

Here is a list of the questions for you to reference when you go to the shop you are interested in. There is also a printable version along with an area for notes available on my website at www.TheHairMint.com.

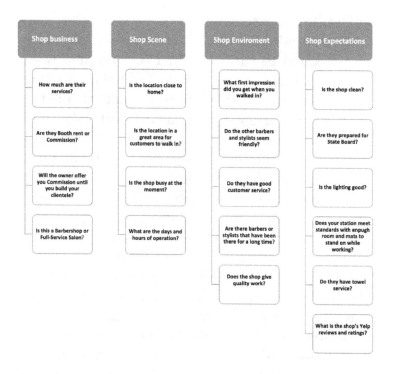

Shop business	Shop Scene	Shop Enviroment	Shop Expectations
How much are their services?	Is the location close to home?	What first impression did you get when you walked in?	Is the shop clean?
Are they Booth rent or Commission?	Is the location in a great area for customers to walk in?	Do the other barbers and stylists seem friendly?	Are they prepared for State Board?
Will the owner offer you Commission until you build your clientele?	Is the shop busy at the moment?	Do they have good customer service?	Is the lighting good?
Is this a Barbershop or Full-Service Salon?	What are the days and hours of operation?	Are there barbers or stylists that have been there for a long time?	Does your station meet standards with enpugh room and mats to stand on while working?
		Does the shop give quality work?	Do they have towel service?
			What is the shop's Yelp reviews and ratings?

Overall, when you go into the shop for the first time, you should be looking for many things. Don't be nervous; just be observant, show your personality, be professional, and take into account everything we discussed.

Finding the perfect shop for you may take a little time, research, and consideration, but it will be worth it. It may be a good idea for you to finish reading this book, take some notes, think carefully about what you expect from the shop you want to work at, and then call around to the barbershops or salons you are considering and narrow it down to your top five places, then go in and talk to the owners. Good luck—you'll do great!

My Shop Experience

When I graduated, I didn't have a plan. All I knew is I wanted to cut hair, but I had no idea what shop I wanted to work at, so I just started going around to a few places. Yelp was not invented at that time, but there were a few barbershops in the area that were popular. At the first location, I actually ran into an old high school friend of mine, and ironically, he was a barber too! When I asked him how the shop was, he told me I wouldn't want to work there because there were a lot of barbers there already and they were struggling for walk-ins. He said that it might be hard for me to get new clients coming straight out of school. So, he recommended me to another shop, not too far away that was fairly new and had more space available. I went and talked to the owners, and this ultimately ended up being my first barbershop. This was a nice urban barbershop with a modern feel in a suburban area. This shop mainly had barbers, but there were a couple of stylists there as well, so I was able to take women clients as well as men. It was such a great experience, and I learned a lot! I learned how to fade, taper, do lineups, texturizers, designs, short hair on women, press n curls, flatiron, and how to take weaves out. The owner was a barber and gifted me with my first pair of Andis Master Clippers. I loved those clippers; they meant a lot to me. It didn't take long for me to realize how special they were; I became infatuated with those clippers and mastered them. I knew how to take them apart and put them back together. My love for this brand fueled my career.

To this day, their tools are amazing and are still my favorite, hands down. I actually ended up working for them some years down the line. (I discuss this later in the book.)

I never put a limit on what I could learn, and I'm not really sure if I knew it then, but that became a very important aspect of my career. I was just operating off of passion, but this is why I'm sharing it with you now, so you can utilize all the opportunities you get to excel in learning everything you can and carry it with you. You will not regret it, I promise!

Although the first shop I worked at was memorable and so much fun, after 4 years it was time for me to go. I realized that I needed more experience and I had reached my limit there. My next location was a local Supercuts. Supercuts is a franchise with over 2,600 locations across the US. Unfortunately, they aren't known for their great haircuts, but they will get you in at a moment's notice with no appointment necessary. They encourage you to complete haircuts in 20 minutes to receive a commission bonus, but they also offer benefits, which was great because when you are an entrepreneur in a regular shop, you are on your own when it comes to any type of benefits. They also offer a lot of training for their employees. I appreciated the training because it did enhance my speed, and I was able to apply their technique to my own, which really set a base for where I start my haircuts, even until this day. Remember, even if you take one lesson or technique from educational classes, training, or someone, it will always make you better at your craft.

However, I did notice that the stylists are mostly just there for the benefits, so they have a lack of passion for cutting hair and most of the employees treat the job like "just a job." Some are in school for another career, so they aren't interested in building a clientele; they are just working part-time, trying to make ends meet. For me, however, I took pride in my work and wanted all my haircuts to look good. I never wanted anyone to say that I did a bad haircut, and if you're serious about this profession neither should you. Not to mention, I planned on having my clients follow me, so customer service and satisfaction meant a lot to me.

Needless to say, I hardly ever made my commission bonus because I took my time and made sure my clients were happy. Eventually, I became a manager, which I enjoyed. My training became more intense and I got the chance to learn the business and the retail side of running a franchise salon, and I got a feel of how it would be to run my own shop and be in charge of employees. At times it was stressful if I had to fix an employee's haircut, but ultimately it improved my skills and allowed me the experience of making clients happy. Overall, Supercuts was a great experience because I learned how to cut a lot of different ethnicities and textures since different types of people came there for haircuts.

Pro Tip: While you are in school and making mistakes, take the time to learn how to fix them. Start taking the time to think through the haircut and figure out what it will take to fix it. If someone else messes up a haircut, offer to help fix it; eventually, you will get good at it. Remember, if you learn how to fix haircuts, you'll learn not to make mistakes, and if you do, you will be able to fix them.

My next location was a full-service hair salon that was mostly hairdressers, except for one barber. This salon was all different ethnicities: White, Filipino, Black, and Hispanic, with an Italian owner. This place was great! I love a place with a variety of people. We had a great flow of clientele from all ethnicities come in that shop and many experienced employees. I built up a lot of clientele, developed a lot of confidence, became fluent in color, and learned a lot about styling hair. I stayed there for a couple of years until the owner decided to sell the shop.

Right before he closed the shop, my co-worker, who was a really good friend of mine, said she was going to buy a salon right down the street and asked if I wanted to come. I did and it was just the two of us until some of the other stylists came a couple of weeks later, and we eventually got a few new stylists as well. I helped out a lot to get the shop up and running, and I learned a lot about opening up a salon from scratch. I watched it grow over the years and had a lot of great memories. The one thing I took from that experience is I learned not to open a shop of your own until you know you are ready to dedicate your life to it. It takes an enormous amount of dedication, passion, and hard work to run a successful shop. I also took some of my biggest steps there and grew so much in the eight years the shop was open. This was in that shop that I made the important decision to focus on myself and put all my energy into me and follow my heart. At this point in my career, I had a lot of loyal clients and the confidence that I was a great barber and could take anyone who walked into the door, so ultimately, it was at this shop that I decided to get more involved with hair shows and eventually go work in LA to pursue the entertainment industry.

After the owner closed the shop, I decided to only keep my closest customers and focus on my LA clients and gigs because I was really getting busy. After a year of being out of the shop, I decided to look for another place because I missed the environment and the love you get from the barbershop. I love how it keeps me fluent with my haircuts and up-to-date with current hair and tool trends. I wanted to find a place my clients would be happy to go to and a shop for me to be in a couple of days a week in between my gigs. I found this wonderful shop near my house that has an amazing owner that I love and a great family environment. I really got lucky and I feel blessed to be there today.

Along with choosing shops that were either a good fit for me or I knew I could increase my skillset, I made sure each move had a purpose and each place had meaning. My intention with every move was to grow my clientele and expand my expertise. I also made sure throughout my entire career I attended classes, hair shows and events that were going on to help me network and stay on top of trends; the goal was to become as great as I could be.

I hope my experiences show that you can achieve growth with every move you make throughout your career. The goal of it all is to make this journey rewarding for both you and your clients. You want to work comfortably in an inspiring environment, make consistent money, and focus on what's important for your business and your clients. Once you start to establish a great flow of clientele, you can start thinking of what you want to create next in this amazing career. Good Luck!

"

...the goal is to grow as a person, be successful, protect yourself and your family, and live comfortably from a business you not only have your heart invested in but that you have built from your passion.

"

Chapter Seven

Being Self-Employed

Being in the hair industry is not like a normal job or career, and I admit I didn't think about anything but cutting hair when I started in this industry. I was young and like most of you, all I was focused on was cutting hair and being the best at it. I knew a little about what it was like to have a regular job, but I had no idea of the importance of having benefits and protection for myself and my future. When I started cutting hair, I didn't even realize that I was actually in business for myself and didn't know what it meant to be self-employed.

Being self-employed comes with a lot of responsibility and you really have to take the time to protect yourself in every way! The last thing you want is for something unexpected to happen to you or your family that causes you to wonder what you are going to do and how you will you make it through these times. Dealing with an emotional tragedy can easily escalate to another level when it becomes financial too. When you are an adult and self-employed, you are now responsible for yourself, your family, and your future. Do not wait until it is too late!

In this business you don't have paid family leave,

sick time, or vacation time like you would if you were employed by a company for a few years. So then what do you do when you get sick or need to take some time off? This is why you have to be prepared for these times. Part of being your own boss is making sure you are taking care of yourself for the times you need it the most and also for your future.

This might seem like a lot to think about, but I promise it will be the best decision you could make for yourself. After all, while I was writing this book during 2020, we—meaning me, you, and the entire world—were going through a pandemic, a virus that made it impossible for us to work safely, and the world as we knew it instantly changed. This is something I don't think any of us saw coming. What did you do when this began? Did you have money saved? Did you panic not knowing what you were going to do next? Did you sacrifice your health and the health of the people around you and continue to work? Did you receive your stimulus money from the government? As you can see this was something so unexpected that it's been hard for everyone, even for the people who were somewhat prepared and had some money saved. This is a very sad time for a lot of small businesses and for a lot of financially unprepared people. Barbershops were closed down twice, and some will never reopen. These are very unforeseen times. Everybody was so unsure about everything and basically living day to day, trying to figure out what was going to happen next. These topics we will cover will help you protect yourself and make you feel a little better prepared if something like this happens again.

Building Your Credit

Before I get into all the things that are important for us to have as self-employed business people, I have to tell you, as a person who has made mistakes, the very first thing I would do is make sure you take the time to learn what your credit score is and work on making it a 720 or higher.

If you don't know what it is or maybe you don't have any credit, take the time to learn; go into your bank, talk to a financial advisor, and ask how you can build your credit and what is the best route for you to take to reach your goal. Having good credit is not about having a bunch of credit cards. It's about having leverage. It's about having options when you need them most. So, if you don't know anything about credit, how to have good credit, or how to keep it, please talk to a professional, and do some research.

If your credit is not great, find out what is on your credit report that is making it go down, prioritize it, and work on resolving the debt. Credit repair companies can help you, or you can research and fix it yourself. You cannot survive these days without good credit, and you don't want to get into a position where you need it and don't have it because it can cause major setbacks. And honestly, who has time nowadays to go backward?

Credit is something that definitely takes time. No matter if you are just starting to build credit or have a credit score you need to work on, this process will take a while, so take the time and start now. There is nothing like financial stability and peace of mind. Times can get hard and also be unexpected, so if worse comes to worst and you need money, you could take out a low-interest loan to stay afloat until you figure out a game plan. Having your credit in good standing is a confidence booster and will help you when you are trying to make decisions that can change your life.

I cannot stress this enough! It will definitely be the smartest thing you can do for yourself. Please, do not wait!

Medical Insurance
So, the first thing we will discuss is medical insurance, especially if you don't have any. Accidents can happen in seconds, and with medical insurance, you will be covered. Medical insurance can be another not so fun bill to pay, but it is necessary. You can look into a few available plans. Some let you choose the deductible; a deductible is a specific amount of money you have to pay out of pocket before your insurance will pay for services. These can be different amounts but aren't usually too high. It depends on your insurance carrier but your policy will also state it.

There are low and no deductible health plans available, but your monthly premium will be higher. There are also high-deductible health plans that have a higher deductible when you have to go to the doctor, but they will have a lower monthly premium. Also, some of these plans offer a health savings account option; this savings account is not taxed and can be used for any unexpected out-of-pocket healthcare costs. There is also a tax deduction on these health insurance premiums for self-employed individuals which will give you added benefits and will reduce the amount you owe in taxes if any. You can always look in your area for a local insurance agent to help you find the best insurance to fit your needs and your budget; you can also ask your tax pro to help you with those tax breaks and help you get the most of those savings.

Accidental Insurance

The next is accident insurance, such as Aflac or Combine Insurance. This is a supplemental insurance that is important to have because you never know when accidents or sickness will happen, and your income suddenly stops because you are unable to work. You can check your local agencies to see what's available in your area. These insurance premiums are often pretty low, depending on the package you decide to pick. But they provide peace of mind in case something unexpected happens and you're unable to work, like a sprained wrist, a twisted ankle, or a car accident. And the benefits are often paid quickly. These insurance policies help with reimbursements of out-of-pocket medical expenses on and off the job and benefits are paid directly to you. So why not be protected and at least have some money coming back to you when you need it most.

General Liability

So, let's talk about protection insurance in case something unexpected happens while you are working with a client. It is important to consider looking into some sort of liability insurance for your protection. This will protect you if something happens to a client while they are in your place of business. General liability covers the costs of physical injuries and damages, and professional liability protects you if they are harmed from a service you provide or advice you give.

Several insurance companies cover our professional trade; there's even an insurance company for barbers called National Association of Barbers Insurance Plus that will provide coverage for slip and falls, facial cuts, unsanitary instruments, stolen equipment, chemical/product reactions, and more! They currently have a rate of $159 per year and it covers a number of benefits from two million per occurrence of professional and general liability, product liability, $100,000 in rental location damage, $1,000 in stolen equipment insurance, $25,000 in identity protection plan and more! They also offer part-time barber insurance and student liability insurance as well. This insurance is pretty much a necessity if you pay booth rent in a shop and are considered self-employed. Don't get caught without it!

Retirement

Paying into your retirement is especially important. You want to think about your future when you are young; the earlier you start, the more comfortably you will live later. The last thing you want to do is turn around and realize you're 40, and think how am I going to live if I have no income or what if something happens ending my career early? Maybe you have health issues, maybe you don't, but your retirement will be here before you know it, and you need time to save for it. Retirement savings must be a priority!

Now is the time to start looking into investment retirement accounts you can start that will enable your money to work for you! There are Solo 401(k), SEP IRA, SIMPLE IRA, Keogh Plan, or Traditional or Roth IRA accounts. Take the time to find a financial advisor or a financial institution that can go over plans and answer any questions you may have before you decide which one fits your needs best. Some companies even offer free or low-cost retirement planning advice to potential clients. So even if you can't afford much at the beginning, the sooner you start, the more you'll accumulate! The bottom line is to GROW YOUR WEALTH!

Saving Tips

Next, you want to start saving money as soon as you can to set yourself up for success later on in life. We as barbers and hairdressers see a lot of money come and go, and we don't always pay attention to where it goes. You would be surprised by how much you actually waste that could be going toward your future to benefit you.

There are a few important things you should be saving for: taxes, retirement, and emergency savings. These are three things you will definitely thank yourself for later when it comes time to need it. Besides making sure your taxes are paid, creating a financial goal for your future, and being prepared for an emergency are very necessary and key to staying on top of your business. Saving for important times or long-term financial goals can be difficult, but it can be done, consider this as investing in yourself and taking care of yourself first.

Being a self-employed barber or stylist can make it hard to be faithful to saving a specific amount each month because our income fluctuates, but there is a solution for that. Saving a certain amount every month or even every week sounds like a good idea but let me explain to you why it is not.

First, when you save a certain amount, you are more likely to miss a savings payment to yourself, because maybe it's a slow week and you feel you didn't make enough or if something comes up and you can't afford to contribute. The first thing you will do is make a promise to yourself to put away double next time, but this promise isn't always possible and could throw you off. Also, the weeks when you are busy and you can afford to put away more, you are still are putting away the same amount. You will not be making the most of your savings this way. Therefore, the key is to stick to a certain percentage: let's say 25 to 30 percent of your earnings for the week to go toward your three goals. Think of this as paying your future self first! This way on weeks you make less, you put away less, and the weeks you make more, you will put away more. You are more likely to be consistent with this because you will be basing your savings off your income and your contributions will match your income for that week.

You will be surprised how much you can save with this pay-yourself-first mindset, and the more you save, the more secure you will feel about your future as time goes on. Another great idea is to look into opening an interest-bearing checking or savings account that will let you make something on the money that you're saving. The only time you will be taking money out of this account is to pay your taxes quarterly, so make sure you are aware of any penalties you may encounter. But no matter what you do, make sure you contribute to your long-term financial goals!

Remember, pay yourself first!

Pay Your Taxes

Earlier we talked about saving to pay your taxes. A lot of barbers and hairstylists I know do not pay their taxes every year; some not at all. I know this is a business you could easily just make the cash and pocket it. I also understand it's not an easy world to make it in financially, but this is all the more reason to have a plan and focus on what's best for you and your future.

I know you are saying, especially with everything going on in this world, why is paying taxes so important? Well for example, during this 2020 Covid-19 crisis, a lot of the barbers I knew that did not pay taxes did not get their stimulus checks. They were waiting and wondering, but they were basically unknown to the government and didn't receive anything. The people who paid their taxes had their checks automatically deposited into the bank account that they used to pay or receive their tax refunds. A few barbers I know chose to file after that, and eventually got their stimulus check. But they may have to make arrangements for the taxes they owed for last year if any. If you have never paid before, and you have a few years accumulated, don't be afraid once you do file of having years of taxes to pay back. After all, you may qualify for penalty relief through special IRS waivers such as First Time Abatement, which can remove penalties for filing and paying late if it's your first offense. There are also other penalty relief options based on your circumstances. So, talk to a tax specialist, ask questions, and see what your options are.

Paying your taxes is important because this pays into your self-employment tax for you later on in life. Self-employment tax is basically a tax consisting of Social Security and Medicare primarily for individuals who work for themselves. Generally, your employer would take these taxes out for you and match your contribution, but when you are self-employed, you have to pay the IRS yourself.

However, the self-employment tax will cost you less than you might think because you get to deduct half of your self-employment tax from your net income. Don't worry—find a good tax person, and they will do this all for you! But think of this as a way of paying into your future. Later, when you're 65 years old, you will have your Social Security benefits to add to your retirement income we talked about earlier. So, if you haven't filed any returns so far and haven't paid your self-employment tax, your earnings for those years won't get counted toward your future Social Security benefits, and this can have a huge impact on your future income and quality of life. Also, while you are entitled to receive your benefits at age 65, if you wait until you're 70, you are eligible for full retirement benefits, so if you chose to wait, your amount will increase. This may seem like a long time away for you if you are a young barber, but let me tell you time flies, and the next thing you know, you will be looking for all of these things we are discussing, and if you want to be well prepared for your future, start early!

Another benefit of paying your taxes is being able to prove your income in case you want to buy your first home, car, or any other big item for yourself. The hardest thing we have as barbers or stylists is proving our income, and this is the way we have to do it. Since we don't receive W-2s from an employer, we have to use our tax documents to prove our income. I do believe that recently, mortgage companies will accept bank account statements from the last couple of years as a form of proof, but you would have to check with your realtor.

But hey, don't let all this become overwhelming; there is good news! Filing taxes doesn't mean that you will necessarily owe the IRS. If you are head of household and have dependents you can claim, more than likely you will get money back! And that can be something you can look forward to having as a lump sum come tax time! Just start saving all your receipts on anything you spend for your business, and be sure to include all the expenses, deductions, and credits you qualify for. The big deductions are health insurance premiums, business insurance (like we discussed earlier), internet and phone, meals, travel, vehicle use, booth rent, supplies (tools and products), education (classes, this book! etc.), retirement plan contributions, advertising, tax preparer fees, and so on. These are some of the main ones but there are more!

I know we have been talking about paying taxes, retirement, and saving for emergencies, and maybe this has worried you, but don't let it! Prioritize these things for yourself and take your time to learn about each of them, one at a time if you have to. You have some time. But one thing I learned, 2020 is the year for educating yourself, being more aware of what is actually going on in your life and in the world, and preparing for your future and the unexpected.

I know things are hard right now for all of us and may seem impossible some months, but if you set up your priorities, focus on what you can do, and set the rest as goals, you will do it! Build your clientele, work hard, make a budget for yourself, be aware of where your money is being spent, and plan ahead. You can do this!

If you are new to the barber or hairstylist world and you are still figuring yourself out, that is okay; just make this a goal to strive for and come back to this chapter later if you need to remind yourself. Like I said, start one goal at a time, but ultimately, in the years to come, the goal is to grow as a person, be successful, protect yourself and your family, and live comfortably from a business you not only have your heart invested in but that you have built from your passion.

SECTION THREE:

BEYOND
THE SHOP

"

The goal is to be successful at your creative vision and live comfortably doing it.

"

Chapter Eight

Starting a New Creative Direction

When you think about expanding your career outside of the shop and turning it into a new creative direction, you should be thinking of how to design a career that has the flexibility to grow with you and can get you to financial independence. The goal is to be successful at your creative vision and live comfortably doing it. This requires investing in yourself, seeking knowledge, and working toward becoming the best version of yourself.

Earlier in chapter three, we talked about healthy habits and how to inspire and maintain your motivation for creativity, so refer back to it whenever you need to. We all need motivation and a creative push from time to time. After being in the hair industry for years, it's only natural to want to take your insight and knowledge in this artistic business to the next level. It takes a lot of focus, determination, and consistency to venture outside the shop to be a creative entrepreneur such as a mobile barber or stylist in various entertainment fields, to starting a business such as a product line, or creating a brand; so just be prepared and take it one step at a time.

There are many paths you can take in the hair industry that can turn into you living out all of your artistic dreams. You are not required to only stick with one, as a matter of fact as you navigate through this creative industry you have the option to become as great as you want! Who knows you may be so inclined to tackle a couple of these accomplishments, your future is yours to manifest. Let's discuss your possibilities!

Be Mobile or Freelance for the Sports, Music, Tv/Film or Agency

There are tons of options to explore in the hair industry, you never know what just one opportunity can bring. It can literally give you life changing possibilities and put you in places you would have never before imagined. I know a lot of barbers and stylists who have chosen to take their talents to different sides of the spectrum from doing hair in exclusive salons for clients that are willing to pay top dollar for a haircut and shave or a cut and color; this is ideal because they never have to travel far to make good money. Or being an on-call barber for athletes of major sports teams from football, basketball to baseball and even golf. The perks of having these types of clients are traveling to where they are if needed, jobs in editorials and commercials and having the access to the games they are playing; not too bad. These barbers most likely started doing one player and it turned into a major hair account (as I like to call it). It only takes one person to come into the shop and your expertise, knowledge and skills can turn that one engagement into a life changing experience.

Along with the Sports Industry, there are a lot of professional industries that are in high demand for mobile barbers such as the Music Industry; this includes artists (male or female) of all genres, that need haircuts, styling, shaves, color, etc. for music videos, editorials, tv appearances, award shows, red carpets and more. Having one artist that is busy can make your schedule demanding and require you to work at a moment's notice and with no days off. Working with these artists you will have frequent jobs such as videos, editorials, talk shows, events and award shows. The perks of having these types of clients is traveling when needed on tour, and having access to concerts and opportunities to meet and work with other artists is highly possible. We go more in depth on this in "The Entertainment Industry" chapter later in the book.

In the Television and Film Industry there are a lot of opportunities to work on a continuous basis working on Talk Shows, or for Television Networks that have consistent shows with continuous seasons. This is great for longevity and is usually pretty easy to obtain another job once one show has ended. These jobs tend to have structured days and times and are usually paid at a rate that complements your experience. Because of the amount of time you spend with the talent, you could end up with a permanent client that will request you outside of set as well. The perks of this job is possibly being recognized for the Make-Up Artists and Hair Stylist Guild Award for Best Contemporary Hair Styling in Television and New Media Series; this award is given out annually. You will also be able to obtain time for the Union, if you decide to join.

In order to be in the Film Industry you have to join the Union. We discuss the Union more in depth as well in "The Business Side" chapter later in the book. The Film Industry can be demanding with long hours and possibly far locations, but the creativity is endless and the experience you get is priceless. The perks of this side of the Industry is you are also considered for The Guild Award for your work, if your movie was an award-winning movie. Plus, the pay and the benefits are not only satisfying, you get to learn all the secrets and the magic of the movie industry and see your work come to life on the big screen!

Just like the Music Industry if you work for an Actor or Actress off set as well you will be on call for all the appearances they have to attend from Award Shows, Premieres, Talk shows, Editorials, readings and parties. The money is good but the convenience of having a barber or stylist come to them for haircuts or beauty services makes for a busy lifestyle. Being a mobile barber or stylist is becoming more popular by the day. The demand for people to maintain their desired look is wanted at all cost, and they will expect for you to make the sacrafices and arrangements to be there when needed.

Along with being a personal barber and stylist to the elite, some prefer to aim their efforts towards working for a reputable top agent who represents Hair and Make-up Artists doing Photoshoots for Editorials, Advertising and Commercials with celebrities for major magazines and brands. If you are a Barber, you may want to consider being a full groomer which is where you would do light makeup for the client as well. This is rare in the Entertainment Business in any aspect; they usually have to hire two people, but if you can manage this it will not only make you more money, it will set you apart from the rest and even better make you more valuable. If you are desiring to join this side of the industry, depending on your experience you may have to be an assistant to a stylist or groomer to learn the ropes before you go on your own. This is the best way to go so you can be confident when the demand of the job in on your shoulders. This may also pave the way for you to gain other experiences you wouldn't otherwise have access too; such as Fashion Campaigns for huge fashion icons and brands. Having an agent that works for a top agency to represent you means they handle the negotiations for top pay, they also create your invoices for all your jobs, and they make sure you have required breaks and are not overworked without compensation. Having this representation has many perks such as high paying gigs with A-list celebrities for top magazines and brands, the opportunity to work with top photographers and the chance for you to continue to work with these celebrities on an ongoing basis. The opportunities are endless, and the experiences are priceless. We discuss this more in depth later in the Business Side chapter.

All of these careers are amazing and if being a mobile barber, stylist or freelancing for any of these industries is something that you want to focus on, here are a few tips to follow!

* Take every opportunity you have to enhance your knowledge, skills, techniques and become versatile with different looks and styles.
* Make sure you are confident and willing with your mindset and able with your skillset.
* Start now to build a portfolio of your best work and be ready to send it when requested.

You can market your services by offering to do house calls to clients who are willing to pay for the accessibility and your talent; even if they are your regular clients! This will give you the opportunity to get use to house calls and what it takes to be prepared when you work in different environments outside the shop. This will help prevent any problems and making mistakes later when it counts!

Remember, we have a special talent which means you can create a special career out of it. Don't forget timing is everything, so trust the process! Prepare yourself along the way and you will be fine when your opportunity comes along. Be fearless when pursuing any of these amazing industries; do not underestimate your superpower!

Next we will talk about starting a business, any business will require taking steps even if it is opening up your own Barbershop or Salon. When creating a business to expand your creative vision, you can go a lot of directions in this industry and the possibilities can be infinite. But regardless of the direction you take, you will need to go through a series of steps so that you can have an idea of where to start. I am hoping these steps can help you toward getting started on creating a path to turn your idea into a reality. This chapter is here for you to reference along your journey of creating your vision. Take notes in the back of the book, write your goals and ideas down, highlight the important steps, take your time, do more research, breathe.

This will no doubt be a lot of work, but ultimately, it will be an extension of your creative dream and your contribution to yourself and this incredible industry you are a part of. You have already invested in yourself when you decided to go to school with your vision to become a barber or stylist. This, too, will be an investment, but it will be so worth it; you are worth it!

Starting a Business
Let's get started. Here is an example.

Let's say you want to express yourself and create

your own quality product you can be proud of, not only to use on your own clients but also share it with the world.

First, you will want to do some research on similar products for ingredients, pricing, bottle type, and labeling, and then decide what you like about it or what you want to change. Write down any ideas or information you have found.

Next, create your plan in steps, it will include your financial strategy (for samples, packaging, creating the product, etc.) business structure along with any permits, insurance, etc., finding a chemist of your choice, length of time to produce your product or to create samples, and testing them. Also, allow time for creative mistakes —we all make them.

After your plan is complete, start the process of creating your product, and once you love it, you will want to do a product run of samples and begin to set your product up for marketing. All of this will take time but it's okay to take your time, enjoy the process, and get it right.

Here are the steps we talked about above in detail, and hopefully this will help give you an idea and insight on starting your next adventure outside of the shop!

Step 1: Come up with an idea and get a feel for what you want to expand in. Be prepared to do your research and find what you love. Keep your eyes and ears open to ideas and new feelings because you have to love it and you have to feel the passion for it in order for you to drive this idea. You have to feel it in your mind and know it in your soul. This goes for any time throughout your life when you create change. This will ensure that throughout the process of bringing your idea to life and after the success, it will never feel like you're working.

Step 2: Create a plan. This plan is almost like making a blueprint of your ideas. You have to visualize your end goal and make a step-by-step written out plan for how you will get there. So, gather all the information you need about your creation and start doing the research. Predict what some hurdles will be and write out how you will get over them. For instance, in the example above you will research all ingredients and pricing, and you will need to find and decide on bottle types and labeling. Figure out what will economically and effectively work for you. Don't forget to write down what you like, any idea changes and information you have found.

Step 3: Plan your finances and get them in order. Go through your plan and write down what all the expenses will be. Be as specific as possible. Do your research to plan for additional expenses that could come up. Look at the costs for licensing permits and insurance. Ask someone who has done something similar if you are forgetting anything. Your financial strategy is important to have in detail from the very beginning in order for your business to be lucrative and successful.

At this point you can start creating your product or idea and preparing it for perfection. This will be a trial and error phase but that is to be expected, be patient. In the meanwhile, you can move on to step 4.

Step 4: When it's time to start your new business, choose a business structure, are you going to be a sole proprietor (independent), a partnership (you have a partner), an LLC, or a corporation? Different entities offer different benefits to your business. You can do a lot of research online for yourself to get an idea of terminology and questions to ask, but talk to a tax person, business attorney, or business advisor to choose the business structure that will fit your business the best.

Step 5: Once you decide on a business structure, pick and register your business name. Do we even need to discuss how important this is? Choosing your new name is vital to your successful business. Think about this intensely. Write some ideas down, have at least two options in case one is taken, ask some trusted friends their opinion, embrace the name, and own it before you choose it. You have to really consider and make sure you are totally happy and satisfied with it because changing it will be a difficult process. Let the name represent you and the direction of your new creative journey. Once you are completely happy with it, go register it and make it official!

Step 6: Get licenses and permits. We talked about this in step three. Depending on what type of business or brand you are planning on starting, you will have to obtain a few required licenses and permits. If you find a professional to help you start your business structure they should also be familiar with any permits or licenses you will need, or you can look up under your city and state and see what is required for your type of business.

Step 7: Although you are used to doing everything yourself you will need other reliable people you trust to help you so get your team together and ready. They will help you with marketing, content curation, and anything that you need so you can focus on creating a great product. This may require time and energy trying to find people that believe in your vision that are very supportive and are just as motivated as you are. These people should be consistent, have a great work ethic, and add value to your business. They should be a genuine asset.

Step 8: Finalize all of your ideas and moves you have made so far. Make sure you have crossed all your t's and dotted all your i's. All of these steps should pretty much complete your process and you should feel good where you are at this point. So, get ready to start promoting your business and watch it evolve!

Step 9: Promote your business and begin marketing. There are several ways to market your product or business. You can make appearances and go to local marketing events and spread the word by introducing yourself and passing out your business cards. These in-person techniques are always good because they give people a sense of your personality and help you seem relatable. But the two ideas we will talk more about are social media marketing and content marketing as they are more popular, current strategies because of the ever-explosive internet craze.

Marketing

The internet makes it easier for you to get your product or newly established business out there into the view of millions without even leaving your home. The internet is the most powerful tool we have these days and is essential to your business. All you need is a camera, a video camera, and internet access. And I mean with all our technology, social media apps, and the phones we have these days, you have all three of these things whenever you need them at your fingertips!

Social media marketing strategies

Marketing with social media has never been easier. Devoting your time to doing a lot of research and taking a few marketing, computer, and business classes would help you on your journey to becoming a successful entrepreneur. There are also new and growing platforms such as Clubhouse that hold conversation rooms that inspire, motivate and give you great insight on starting a business, marketing it, or making your current ideas or endeavors successful. Remember knowledge along with your mindset is key to prosperity. No one can take away your education, so why not empower yourself?

Clubhouse is a new platform but creating a marketing strategy based on Instagram alone might be one of the best ways to not only gain new customers and spread the word about your product or service but will also cost you nothing but your time and effort. This makes networking and marketing your product easy from the comfort of your home or on the go. I'm pretty sure you plan on using social media platforms for marketing yourself, new product, brand, or service, so here are some strategies and outlets to help you create your online presence that is only a few clicks away.

You should plan on exploring more than just Clubhouse or Instagram which is linked to Facebook, but also Snapchat, YouTube videos, and the ever-growing popular Tik Tok. These sometimes go hand in hand, with links to connect from one to the other. And with the popularity of these social media outlets, you can take your product to the next level in no time. You can use these to focus on main points or the characteristics of your product, or any aspect of your business that you want your customers to focus on. This will also help create a brand for your company. This allows you to introduce something new or explain in detail the specifics of your product or what your company has to offer, and they should be able to find you on every platform. Because social media is diversifying, you should think about which social media platform, if not all, will be the most beneficial to your company or brand.

Social Media is crucial to the success of your product, idea, company or brand. As a new or existing business owner, you will have a lot of other responsibilities that need your attention, so you will be performing multiple tasks a day. This may not be a good idea. Focusing on more than one major task can lead to nothing getting effectively done. Keeping up with promoting your business on all of your social media outlets can become a great deal of work. You should definitely be hands on and aware of what your business needs are to ensure success, and also oversee any decision that needs to be made, but if it begins to be too much, don't get overwhelmed, give some of these duties to the team you structured.

Branding

Branding is different than creating a company, it makes a statement that represents your company, like a recognizable logo, symbol, or name. Let's take Nike for example, when you see the swoosh, you know it is Nike. Creating a brand is a global term and has everything to do with strong marketing. It's important to establish this as early in your career as you can, especially if you are the brand! However, if it is your business or creation the key is to do it with specific branding in mind. What type of characteristics or voice do you want your company to have? Your brand's voice should be similar to a personality. You want it to feel relatable. Ask yourself, what does your company sound like? What does it value? What problems does it solve? Your company needs to have its own voice and sound, and the goal is to be recognizable to your customers or potential customers on social media. You want people to expect this sound or voice from your company, and you want this sound or voice to be associated with your brand every time. So put your creative cap on and start brainstorming — what will it be? Remember, every piece of content you create whether its text, image, or video should match your branding goals.

This is important to think about from the start, so you have an idea where to direct your product or company's attention. You want your company to stand for something and speak volumes without even saying anything. You want it to be recognizable and trusted just by seeing the logo. This takes dedication and powerful marketing, and most of all, consistency and time. Your brand will ultimately represent you, so what do you stand for?

I know this is a lot of information, especially if you are just dipping into the idea of starting your brand or business, or barely stepping into the hair industry for that matter, but it gives you something to think about, and I say why not have the information there when you need it or are ready and have a little head start.

You are an amazing, creative entrepreneur to have entered this industry in the first place, so don't be nervous to move forward and take any of these options to the next level. Take it one step at a time, start small, don't rush into it, think it through, and enjoy the entire journey from beginning to end. You are your own brand the minute you decided to join the hair industry, but more so when you chose to step outside of your comfort zone and explore all of your career goals. No matter what choice you make you, your idea, product, service, company, or brand will be a reflection of you. Trust me, when the time comes, it doesn't matter which avenue you choose, your passion will drive you and your anticipation for success will take control. This will be a remarkable and exciting time for you, and you will be so proud to watch yourself or your creation evolve. Like this book is for me, in so many ways it will be the most rewarding journey you will ever take!

"

…being a creative is powerful and we thrive through constant inspiration.

"

Chapter Nine

Hair Shows

Another creative adventure to consider is Hair Shows! The years I spent on that stage changed my life! It was definitely an exciting part of my experience as a barber. I spent 2 years trying to get involved, and it paid off. The confidence I had in myself and my talent was unstoppable, I decided to start going to hair shows because of my love for cutting hair. I encourage you to go as well; these shows are always an experience and have the newest tools and different types of classes to take. When I first started cutting hair, I realized that being a creative is powerful and we thrive through constant inspiration. I was always saving my money and taking the time out of my schedule to enjoy all three days of walking around watching demos, taking classes and buying all the newest tools. I looked forward to going to hair shows every year, I was very excited to learn and couldn't wait to become better, so I would attend every show I could.

Hair shows, also known as beauty trade shows, are typically spread out over a few days and bring together barbers and hairstylists from all over. They are filled with new products, celebrities, influencers in the industry, tons of sneak peeks, educational classes, and connections you couldn't get anywhere else! Because of the pandemic this year in 2020 only a few scheduled shows held virtual events for networking and educational classes; this is definitely a change from what we are used to.

On the West Coast in Southern California, we have one major show called International Salon and Spa Expo (ISSE), also frequently called The Long Beach Expo. This is the largest cash-and-carry professional beauty event on the West Coast that provides endless inspiration to boost the attendees' careers and creativity. The show celebrated its 20th anniversary in January 2019. During my years of doing this show, 2008–2013, it mainly focused on hair, skincare, and beauty; it was fun, but it was mostly for hairstylists. Only a small portion was dedicated to barbering which came from two of the biggest clipper companies, Andis and Wahl. Similar shows are The Beauty Experience in Las Vegas, International Beauty Show in NYC, America's Beauty Show in Chicago, and Premiere in Orlando, Florida.

These larger shows usually have tons of classes available from almost every distributor; some are paid, and some are free. Classes consist of haircutting, styling, product knowledge, and hands-on workshops. Andis and Wahl Clipper Companies hold quite a few classes, teaching different tools, techniques and answering questions at select times throughout the day.

There are also large booths and stage shows going on simultaneously throughout the venue. These shows tend to be exciting with tons of people, music blaring, and an endless number of products and tools for sale.

There are only a couple of barber shows that are available to attend, and they are CT Barber Expo in Hartford, CT, and Behind the Chair in San Antonio, Texas. These shows not only have the top clipper companies and barber brands to see, it's a great opportunity to take classes, network within the barber community, and attend or enter a barber battle. A newer Hair Show to hit the scene would be BarberCon, who will have 3 shows scheduled in 2021 in Austin TX, NYC and Los Angeles (Make sure you check for any schedule changes).

On a smaller scale, you have hair shows that are held in hotel ballrooms in different cities. The space is very limited, but they do have quite a few companies that hold demos of haircutting and styling. Although they sell pretty much everything for hair, they don't bring out tons of products or tools because space and sales are limited.

These shows are mainly distributors and local companies that will only bring out their highest selling products and tools. These smaller shows usually hold barber battles and hair competitions. Back in the day, these battles would draw a lot of barbers from all over, either attending to watch or entering to win. I had the opportunity for a few years to be a judge from Andis and hand out awards to the winners.

I was always excited to do this; I saw a lot of talented barbers from all over come out and be amazing. It was fun and inspiring to witness all the talent and to be a judge for a company I loved and for a career I had so much passion for, and I have to say, I was honored to do it! These shows were once a year in Los Angeles and also in Northern California. All of these shows, including the larger ones, were in about five different cities up and down the West Coast as well as in Las Vegas and Arizona. To this day, the shows in Long Beach and Vegas hold the reign for being the largest hair shows on the West Coast. I always loved going to any of the shows and soaking up as much knowledge as I could. At one of the hair shows, I actually attended the same clipper class three years in a row, and I learned something new every single time.

As I went to the same show every year, I started to get to know some of the people who worked there because I would frequent the same booths to see what new tools were out. I began to know some of the distributors from different companies that managed some of the booths as well. One distributor I met was from a company called Hot Tools; they had hairdryers, curling irons, flatirons, and styling tools. After seeing me there often and talking to me every year, he asked me if I would like to get on the platform and demo the tools to show people how to use them and answer any questions they may have. Although my love was for barbering and my passion was to work with Andis Clipper Company, I was not going to turn down any opportunities. I was nervous at first, but I loved it! After that first day, I offered my services to him whenever he needed a stylist. I eventually began to do all the shows with him from Long Beach to the smaller shows in Los Angeles all the way to Las Vegas. I learned a lot from him and gained a lot of confidence and experience on stage interacting and talking to people. I worked for him for about four years in total. It was a lot of work, but we had a lot of fun.

Being at all the shows allowed me to meet and talk to a lot of people from a lot of different companies. As I mentioned earlier, I was given a pair of master clippers that I fell in love with, which ultimately made me fall in love with the company and all of their tools. Working for Andis Clipper Company was a dream job of mine, and I would always make my way over there to watch their platform artists do haircuts and answer questions, and before the show ended, I would purchase each and every new tool they released.

I was approached about working for Wahl, which is a huge clipper company and longtime competitor of Andis. They were looking for a platform artist, and I was recommended. They told me if I was interested to give their office a call. I thought about it and hesitated because I really wanted to work for Andis. I wanted to wait for them because I believed in these tools like I believed in myself. It was all I had ever used since the beginning of my career. And to be honest, I knew everything about Andis's tools and nothing about Wahl.

After much consideration, I did reach out to them, and I turned in an application and portfolio. To my surprise, Lance Wahl, the company's global vice president of professional products, reached out to me and offered me a position as a platform artist. I knew that if I took this job my chances of working with Andis would be very slim. Like I said, they are huge competitors in the clipper industry, dating back to the beginning of both companies. However, I accepted the invitation and I was set up to watch a class that another female barber was instructing so I could see how it was supposed to go. Although my passion was to work as a barber at hair shows, my bigger passion was to work for the company of my choice. This day made me realize that I was there for the wrong reasons. I didn't feel as though I was following what I believed in, so at the end of the day, I turned the job down in hopes of one day working for Andis.

Two years later, with more inquires and two more job applications with portfolios, I finally got the chance to come to a show and fill in for a weekend with Andis! I was so excited and proud to be there! But I was really nervous. It was definitely a challenge because the stage was a lot bigger than what I was used to, and many barbers were coming to the booth to watch and ask questions, so I couldn't act as if this was my first time up there. I had to do a great job on every haircut plus answer questions correctly because all eyes were on me, and there was no time for mistakes. This first day was very intimidating and exhausting, but I was so grateful, and I couldn't believe I finally had the opportunity to work for a company that I had waited so long to work for. My first day was long and tiring, and the weekend was even longer.

It was so much busier and more intense than what I was used to. It was nonstop, but I have to say that the two years leading up to this moment, working on stage, really helped prepare me for all of it. It was almost the same —just on a larger scale. At the time of my hiring, I was still working for my distributor, and my schedule became too hectic to do both. He understood and was happy for me. It was time for me to move on.

When I officially got hired for Andis, they flew me to Wisconsin to train, sign paperwork, and to see the headquarters. I had to learn about all their tools (which I was pretty familiar with already) and how to properly present them on stage and how to sell them. I worked three-day weekends in Long Beach, Los Angeles, Seattle, Las Vegas, and Arizona. It was always fun and challenging but hard work as well.

When I did platform work, I had to find models to cut and demonstrate different tools in our line and be able to inspire and educate people that stood around the stage. I had to keep their attention and try to get them to expand their tool collection. Aside from stage presence, finding a model to demonstrate on was always the hardest part. The type of model I was looking for depended on what tool I was using and what type of haircut I would be doing. People were already showing up to hair shows looking their best, so this was often a task, but it always worked out.

When I was doing the haircuts in front of the crowd, I had to explain every step and answer any questions they had about my technique or the tool I was using. I had to be savvy with my words, and even though I had my favorite tools I loved to use, I had to be familiar with every tool we had and know them all like the back of my hand. This is why it is so important to know different styles and how to cut all textures and types of hair because to do these hair shows, you really have to be versatile and be able to strut your skills and talent confidently. Even though I felt confident in my cutting skills, I was still a little intimidated and nervous because I was in front of a bunch of creative individuals who were looking for all the answers and perfect haircuts every time.

If this is one of your goals, you will have a lot of fun and become very experienced. Along with platform work, you will also be doing floor work. This involves talking to customers who are barbers, stylists, and students, answering all their questions about all tools and products. Over a three-day weekend, you will sell tons of tools and products, and on the last day, you will help clean up and pack up anything that didn't sell. It can be exhausting because you will be standing on your feet, talking, and running around for about a 10- to

12-hour day, but you will be able to add every tool the company makes to your arsenal, travel, and meet a lot of great creative people. Even though all of this makes for hard work and an extremely long weekend, it is also very rewarding.

"

*It's nobody else's fault if you don't
fulfill any of your goals or passions
no matter how unreachable they may
seem.*

Chapter Ten

The Entertainment Industry

This is a chapter that is very, very special to me. Being involved in the entertainment industry has been the biggest, most life-changing experience of my entire life. It has changed and enhanced my life in so many ways; it is really unbelievable. I love what I do and who I do it for and wouldn't change it for the world. It gets tough at times with a lot of and ups and downs and many valuable learning experiences, some harder than others for sure. It has literally tested my faith, integrity, and the confidence that I had in myself, but through it all, it has made me so much stronger, smarter, and confident than I have ever been or could have imagined being. To be in this industry, you have to be driven, hardworking, resilient, and very dependable. You will be making sacrifices in almost every aspect of your life. It is a lifestyle that is unpredictable with very little sleep and little to no vacations. However, it is also the most amazing, exciting, rewarding, gratifying, and enriching job ever!

Surrounding yourself with the right people

There are a lot of things to expect from this industry. Life can and will be hectic, and it's important to remember that your time becomes the most valuable thing you have. You will be spreading your time between work, family, and if your lucky, a social life with your friends. You will go through a lot with the people you love; some will be in your corner rooting for you, but to your surprise, some will also be unsupportive. With limited free time, you will realize that you will need to be picky and choosy about who you spend your time with and who you give your energy to.

For myself, I don't have much time to spend with too many people outside of my family, but I do enjoy being around like-minded people who carry the same type of work ethic and who are striving for great achievements. They don't necessarily have to be in the same industry but knowing you're not the only one with a hectic schedule and goals you are trying to reach makes it seem not too impossible. It's quite the creative push to see or hear of someone that is just as determined as you are accomplishing their goals, and that helps you stay on track to accomplishing yours. Inspiring each other is what we are here for regardless of our end goal.

These types of people always tend to exchange good empowering energy and help me turn my stress into creativity. In this industry, your job will become your priority, and even though you will spend a lot of time alone, this doesn't mean you have to feel alone in your own journey. This happens to be when you learn the most about yourself and are also able to get your thoughts in order. But whenever you get the opportunity to be around some of the gifted people you work with or someone who is on a similar mission, take advantage of it to help fuel your own productivity. You will have a lot of responsibility coming from all directions, but you will also have a great opportunity to be just as great as the people you surround yourself with.

How I Got Started in the Music Business:
People always ask me how I made it into this industry, so I think that sharing some of my experiences will help you understand what this industry entails and how much dedication it takes to work in it. I started with one goal, achieved it, and went to the next. With each goal, I was driven by passion. I had no fear of attaining what I wanted and no doubt I could do it; I just knew it would be a matter of time. Although I have achieved most of my aspirations, I still feel there are other accomplishments I want to achieve. Having the desire to achieve greatness in your life, no matter what aspect, is important because we should always strive to grow as a person and be the best version of ourselves we can be.

Do not limit yourself in this limitless world.

<u>From the Shop</u>
While working at the barbershop, doing stage

work at hair shows, and just starting to work for Andis Clipper Company, I was also thinking about pursuing the entertainment industry to work for music artists; to cut them and their entire teams. I felt like I had enough experience and I was ready for the challenge. This was a rapidly growing industry, especially within rap, and I knew I would be able to evolve in it and start a whole new career for myself. This dream and goal was becoming more and more vivid in my mind. The more I thought about it, the more I knew I could do it.

I lived and worked in a barbershop about 60 miles east of Hollywood and had no idea how I was going to accomplish this idea. Not to mention, I was very focused on doing hair shows as often as possible while in between I was also doing private classes for Andis at barbershops and hair schools throughout Southern California. I was also taking business classes at a community college part-time near my house, as well as being part-time at the shop. I was very busy, but I loved it.

During my promotion for my cutting classes, I met a guy who was a promoter for a nightclub, and he also managed a barbershop in the Mid-Wilshire area in LA. We had a meeting about doing a class at his barbershop, and during the conversation, he offered me a booth at his shop and told me he would do commission if I was interested. I thought about it for a couple of weeks because it was definitely going to be a sacrifice for me to travel out there with no guarantee that I was going to make any money in a new environment with no clientele. But I knew I wanted to get into the entertainment industry and work for music artists. I figured they would need the convenience of a mobile barber for videos, interviews, and performances they had. To do this, I knew I would have to put myself near the area I wanted to work in. So, I took him up on his offer to work at the shop.

When I shared my plans with the owner of the shop where I worked, who was also a friend, she told me that working in entertainment isn't all that it is cracked up to be, and I was wasting my time. She also said if I was going to do that, I needed to come off of part-time and start paying full booth rent for the week. I was surprised and a little thrown off: I would still be there on the same days and hours. She said it was because I would be making more money. I said, "I don't even have any clients out there yet," shortly after, the conversation was over. I knew I didn't have all the answers and I was taking a risk, but I also knew what I wanted and I was willing to make the sacrifice. I wasn't going to let anything deter me. I figured I would just deal with that later. I absolutely know now that, if I had let that discourage me, I would not be where I am today, and more than likely, I probably wouldn't have written this book. So, I will take all the credit for that!

I share this story because I'm proof that you shouldn't let anybody stop you from going after your dreams. It's nobody else's fault if you don't fulfill any of your goals or passions no matter how unreachable they seem. You have to take all the responsibility for not only all of your successes but your failures as well, and although some are hard to take, failures are going to teach you resilience and allow you to grow in the most unique ways. You don't want to regret later in life not pursuing something because of fear or lack of support. Just make sure you are making safe decisions with good intentions that will help you grow as a person. Being the best version of yourself is always the goal.

To the Industry
It didn't take long for me start gaining new clients, and six months later I ended up catapulting myself right into my aspiration of being in the entertainment industry. Although I was new there, I was always ready to work and before I knew it business took off and I have been on the move since. I was on call, running from set to set, studios and house calls for several major artists. Being on-call and traveling to private locations became essential. Grooming became more in demand and having someone available who they could trust to meet their grooming needs, no matter where they were, even if it was just a haircut, was becoming more and more necessary. It quickly became required for me to be available 24 hours a day, seven days a week, so keep this in mind if you want to be involved in this industry. My life continues to revolve around theirs to where I have to take my dinner to go just to meet their needs

promptly or wake up out of my sleep at 2 a.m. to do a last-minute house call. Taking time to myself is nonexistent and vacations, if I can manage to take one, needs to be planned around their upcoming schedule. This is a phenomenal job that allows you to be surrounded by amazing people, incredible energy, and mind-blowing situations. Just know, you will sacrifice a lot for it.

Sean is my Kanye

Although I only worked at the shop in LA three days a week, one night my co-workers and I were at the shop late to clean up after watching the Lakers' game. Around midnight a guy came in with his friend and said, "Can I get a haircut?" Once I started cutting his hair, we started having a conversation about what it is we do. He told me he just moved out here and he raps, and I shared that I wanted to work on sets and cut artists' hair, so if he ever needed anyone, I could do it. I finished him up and gave him my number. A couple of days later, he called me close to midnight (again) as I was heading home and said, "Are you going to be in that shop you were at tomorrow morning? I have an interview I'm doin' and just want to get cleaned up."

I said, "No, I'm only in there a couple of days a week, but where are you now?"

He told me, and I happened to be a couple of blocks away. He sent me the address, so I turned the car around and headed over. That night was the beginning of my career in the entertainment industry. My career grew alongside his, and his incredible work ethic was an inspiration to me. I believe I was meant to be in the shop that night, and he was meant to come into my life and make everything that I had been asking for happen. This is exactly what happens when you manifest something that you believe in with no doubt and no fear. Ironically, he actually taught me that about four years later, and I realized that that is exactly how we met. It always amazes me when I think of that day and where I was in my life. I am forever grateful for that moment. We were both new in this industry and we both worked extremely hard to get where we are today. I watched him build his entire career himself. He worked sick or not, and therefore, so did I. We did what we had to do for our passion with no questions asked. I was there every time he needed me no matter what. He inspired me tremendously, and we had so much in common because, although we had a different goal, our dreams matched.

Throughout the time we worked together, he introduced me to everyone he knew as his barber and told them if they ever needed one to let him know. Although I built a lot of my own relationships along the way, he was always very supportive and opened many doors for me. He gave me my start by believing in me, and I will always appreciate and love him for that. He will always, no matter what, be family to me. We went on to do tons of music videos, TV shows, red carpet events, and editorials for some of the biggest magazines, concerts, and more!

The Most Important Rules

With this highly demanding job, you must understand the rules that come with this industry. You have to learn how to keep things in perspective and understand how to handle situations in order to maintain your credibility. Being a celebrity barber is not an easy profession. I understand it looks fun from the outside, and don't get me wrong, it is an extraordinary job, but it is also a job that requires a ton of commitment and the mindset to be prepared for anything. There are a lot of rules that are set in place and traits you should carry in order to maintain your job.

Four of the biggest traits to develop and rules to understand in this industry are loyalty, the ability to separate your personal life and work life, the ability to not take things personally, and good work ethics.

Loyalty

Not only does this job take sacrifice, but it also takes loyalty. An artist trusting you is one of the biggest compliments. They need to trust not only that you will make them look good, which is a major part of it, but also that they can allow you to be around their personal life. You will be in their home, around their friends and family, and may hear private conversations and music that hasn't been released yet, so loyalty and trust are essential in your relationships with them. Respecting their privacy and space is of utmost importance in this business. If you want to keep your job, remember this is rule number one! You may have to sign an NDA (Non-Disclosure Agreement) before you start working with your client; this is an agreement you sign to not discuss, photograph, or repeat anything you see or hear, but whether your client has an NDA or not, you should treat all of your clients with the same respect to their privacy.

Never invite any friends or even family with you until you are absolutely positive it is okay to do so, and you may even want to give them a heads up and ask before just to see what kind of response you get. You never know what is going on or who may be over there. Don't forget this is your job, and they are your boss.

Do not take pictures without permission or post any content that is being filmed, most of the time you are not allowed to video or take pictures while on set, but if you do happen to take some, you shouldn't post them until it is okay to do so. I rarely post pictures of my clients unless it's of my work, and I always wait until he posts them first.

Do not give addresses out, ever! Giving out their address without permission violates not only their privacy but their health and safety. For example, resist the temptation to tell a rideshare driver who you are headed to see; I have been in some where they will spark up a conversation to figure out what you do and what you are headed to do. At all costs keep your client your priority; their privacy and safety are paramount. There are a lot of rules and regulations in this industry to commit to, but they are mostly common sense; it's always best to first consider what is in the best interest of your client.

Another word of advice—never tell your clients' business to another artist you work with or to anyone else for that matter. If you start telling them someone else's business, they may think you are telling theirs as well. As a matter of fact, if you can help it, keep the business that you do with other artists to yourself. You may think it's reputable and cool to tell an artist that you work with, that you work with a lot of other artists or where you might be going next, but in reality, especially if you are just starting to work with someone, I suggest you keep what you do and who you do it for to yourself because some of them just like the fact that you are there for them and are not interested in who else you are around. Plus, believe it or not, not all artists get along, and they might feel like you could go and tell their business because they don't know you that well yet.

It is better in any situation to stay neutral in these matters and just be there to give great service, build your credibility, and do your job. Another big issue is to never talk about the music any of them are working on to other people; they most likely don't want what they are working on or have coming out to be discussed with other people. That is theirs to share.

Separate your personal life and work life
The first thing I learned in this industry was to

keep your personal life and your business life separated. Once I learned that it wasn't a good idea to mix them, I began to keep them totally separate. I quickly found out that it's just easier to keep them apart, otherwise it will put you in situations you would rather not be in, so I can keep my business and the business of my clients private. It's understandable that some people like to ask questions but it's important for you to respect your privacy and the privacy of your client.

In the beginning, you will want to share all of the exciting moments you were involved in. As this becomes your everyday life, problems or situations will happen that you will want to discuss with someone close to you, but I suggest you don't. This is part of respecting your clients' confidentiality, and since these work issues are not average problems, they will always be new and intriguing to who your telling. Additionally, there is no benefit to telling them as they will never see your problem or have a solution because they don't understand a life they can't imagine, and they are too focused on who it is about than to understand there's even a problem.

It can be hard to share things about the entertainment industry with people outside of it because they are often unable to look at things from a practical point of view. This can make you feel like no one understands, and you can often feel alone. But because of all the people you work around and the work ethic you develop, you will come to realize that this just comes with the industry you are in, and you have to respect it.

For example, when you receive a call for a haircut in the middle of the night and you're asleep, you have to get up and go. This is very common. In this industry, we all work hard at all times of the day or night, and we do what we have to do to make sure things get done. Often, someone would ask me why I was so tired and I'd say, "I had to work in LA last night, I got home at five this morning", and they would say "You're crazy. I wouldn't be going to LA, staying out all night, hope it was worth it." It just seems like very few people actually understand the work ethic that is involved. And yes, it is worth it, but it's also your job, and it just shows that this job isn't for everybody.

Unfortunately, entitlement or the misunderstanding of you not being able to include certain people into your work life, can bring about hurt feelings, so be prepared to lose some people in the process, this is normal; it's hard for people to adjust to a life you are choosing to live that can't always involve them. It can get difficult at times, but everyone in this industry has sadly experienced this at one point or another, but just stay focused, keep moving forward, and try not to take it too personally. It will all work out.

You will also be involved in a lot of private moments with the clients that are not yours to share. As this becomes part of your life, people are always going to be curious and want to know what is going on. At times they will ask questions, but remember, this is your job, and like we discussed earlier, your clients' privacy is a priority, so keep it short and as simple as possible. Sometimes people will choose to go and discuss you and your work life with others and you just don't know what they are going to say. For me, it became easier to just not discuss it or I downplay any situations I'm in for the sake of my privacy, not just my clients'. In a lot of ways, having my privacy always made things easier for me. I learn the less people know the better. Once in this industry, you never know who genuinely wants to be your friend for you or who wants to be your friend to hopefully be around the people you know.

Don't take anything personal!

There will be a lot of times that you will want to take things personally, and sometimes things are personal because they mean a lot to you. After all, this is your hard work, dedication, and livelihood. But one thing I have learned from someone who meant a lot to me and that I still live by today is "No matter what happens to you, good or bad, it is always what's best for you!" And I know that can be hard at times to believe, but if you can always say that to yourself every time something didn't go as planned, you will find that you will handle things better and save yourself a lot of grief. You will be surprised how often we are hard on ourselves for something that we have no control over. I had a client who I worked with for six years who I loved very much and truly enjoyed working with. But one day, he just stopped working with me. Maybe I will never understand why, and often I blamed myself. When these things happen in this industry, it's often quick and with no explanation, so it can really make you doubt yourself. But right or wrong, it won't change anything. You just have to pick up and keep moving. You have to believe in the type of person you are and know you have always done things to the best of your ability.

However, always remain loyal and continue to make sacrifices for your career. At the end of the day, there are no hard feelings. Unfortunately, this is common and ultimately, it was no longer for me nor did it need to be a part or play a role in my life any longer. Shortly after, I began to start working more with new clients and traveling more, and I realized that not working for him opened up the time for me to commit to these new opportunities. If I would have continued to work with him, it would have put me in different places and positions that weren't going to fit my schedule and wasn't best for me at the time.

On the other hand, let's say you have worked with a client one time and you are hoping to continue to work with them, you see that they are in town and you didn't receive a call. There could be other scenarios as to why you didn't receive a callback. Maybe they got a haircut before they came, or maybe they didn't need one while they were in town, or maybe they don't work with the same manager, so they don't have your contact information. Maybe they have a barber or groomer out here already, or maybe they didn't like your work. Regardless, it's not meant for you and that's okay. Just keep working hard and what will be for you, will be.

I work with a few production companies and a few major record labels. They call me for jobs they know I can do and they trust me with. Although I feel comfortable doing anyone and I know I have the skillset for it, they don't always call me for every job they have, and that's okay. I'm sure they have their reasons. It doesn't always have to work out to my advantage. I appreciate all the opportunities they give me, and I show up on time and do my best work possible. Since we don't always know the reasons we weren't called for a job or given an opportunity, there's no reason to feel discouraged. Taking things personally can break your confidence. It's easier to just take these situations as learning lessons, enjoy the process, become great, and count your blessings!

Work ethics
Your work ethics are pretty intense with this type of job, so it is essential for you to be reliable, dedicated, and disciplined. It is very unpredictable and requires last-minute schedule changes and unexpected travel. It is sometimes very hard to manage and can feel impossible at times, especially if you have more than one big artist. They are usually all busy and at different times. Luckily, 90 percent of the time I could juggle four big artists at the same time with insane schedules and still work

at the shop in between. I have to tell you though, if you do this, you will be working every single day with no days off. Literally. Sometimes you might think you finally have a day off, and you get a call for an artist or one of your artists calls and you have to go; I mean you have to go, because being dependable can make all the difference in attaining or keeping your clients. It's not always easy to be available every single time they call, and you will probably be moving things around to make it happen. But when the time comes, and it's out of your control, and you can't make it, it will be understood—if it rarely happens, so you have to make sure this does not occur often because they may really like you and you may do a great job, but if you are not dependable, they will have to use someone else. That could very well be the end of your job. I learned that the hard way.

I had a client who I started with when he was a new artist. I was with him for about two years. I did house calls for him, and we did a couple of videos. Every time he needed me, I was there, but as he became busier and busier with new projects coming out, I was working with a lot of other artists and my schedule was packed. He called me for a haircut at least eight times, and I couldn't go. Granted these calls were at the last minute, and I couldn't arrange my schedule to make it, but it still needed to be done. I explained to him that I really wanted to be there and that he couldn't call me at the last minute because my schedule is too crazy to adjust at the last minute and I also needed time to be able to make it there. During this time,

I ran into him late one night in the studio at two in the morning when I was there setting up to cut another client, and he walked in and said, "What the f#!k!"

I said, "I told you my schedule is crazy. I know I'm fired."

"You're not fired; you're the best, T."

Relieved, I said, "Look, the next time you call me I'm going to drop what I'm doing and come."

He called me about a week later and I couldn't go; I was snowed in, in Pittsburgh, PA, with one of my other clients. I was so upset, but what could I do? He never called me again; understandable. Now he is a huge artist, and I am such a fan and wish I still worked with him. I see him around every now and then, and there are no hard feelings, but he now has his team established. I still hope to get another opportunity to work with him again. We will see. This is how important it is to be available no matter what, and yes, in this situation I couldn't have possibly made it, but I shouldn't have let it get this far. I should have made the sacrifice sooner because there are only so many times you can be unavailable. Things in this business need to keep moving, and they will move with or without you. Do not take your opportunities for granted! Try to plan your schedule out to the best of your ability, and if you have something coming up, make sure you make management aware that you are already committed to certain dates. If possible, offer solutions and try to work it out.

Your schedule will get crazy, and things may need to be moved around, especially if you are still working in a shop. Make sure your shop clients know your schedule could change, and most of the time, they will work with you; just know, you may have to make sacrifices from time to time for them, too.

I remember when I had a day scheduled at the shop and a day off planned as well, and I was in Atlanta heading home. I had another client who needed a last-minute haircut. He had a flight from California to New York, and by the time I would have made it back to California, he would have had to leave, so they bought me a new flight and I had to meet him in New York. Instead of going home like I thought, I was now going to New York for a few days. There went my much needed day off, and I had to rearrange my schedule at the shop. This is a typical day in my life, but as crazy as my life gets, it always works out for me, and I feel blessed to be able to be in demand.

If you want to aspire to be in the same shoes, I encourage you to follow your dreams. You will have a lot of work ahead of you so just make sure you stay consistent, focused, grounded, and dedicated in order to maintain a solid work ethic.

Making it work

Making your schedule work for you can be tough in this business. You have to maintain control of a lot of aspects of your business and personal life to make it all come together smoothly. We will discuss maintaining your schedule with your shop and private clients and dealing successfully with the pressures of the industry.

Maintaining Shop and Celebrity Clients

We just discussed how accessible and dedicated you have to be to your exclusive clients and how it can be chaotic at times maintaining every aspect of your life. I feel that even though you don't get much downtime, it is still important to hold on to all your clients regardless if they are at the shop or part of your private clientele. I have always continued to work at the barbershop while traveling and working with my artists. I have regular clients who depend on me to cut their hair as well. Some I've had since before I began working in the entertainment industry. They saw me go after my goals, achieve what I wanted to do with my life, and have supported me along the way. I appreciate them, and I love working at the barbershop I am at.

People always ask, –Why do you even work at the shop if you have all these celebrity clients? – Well, I do it for a lot of reasons. First of all, I love the culture of the barbershop, and I still get a lot of my inspiration from there. It allows me to keep up with what goes on in the barber world, and it keeps me fluent in my haircuts and also what hair trends and tools are current. I also love the people I work with and the family we have created there. As hard as it gets at times to fit everything into my schedule, I wouldn't give it up for anything. I get my normalcy from the shop. I love it, and it is very special to me. I keep it as separate as possible from my Hollywood life, and I like it better this way. I have realized through the glam of it all, I am an introvert and love a quiet life as well. Plus, I have a pretty good base of clients there that over the years have become like family to me, and it's also very consistent, so I make it work in between my Hollywood clients and traveling.

If you decide to follow this path, try to stay humble and keep your chair at the shop because you can always rely on the shop, and there will always be people that need to have haircuts on a more frequent basis. Yes, you are charging your celebrity clients more, but your shop clients are consistent. If you can swing doing both, do it! In this industry, you are not guaranteed to be with an artist forever. I've seen that change from one day to the next, and their schedule goes through different phases as well. For instance, they may be recording an album for a year and just need haircuts from time to time. But then that album releases and they begin promo, so they will be busy and need haircuts more often. Or they could go on tour and just decide to fly you out when they need a haircut, which is usually on an approved schedule. So, it really just depends on the artist and their needs. An artist may or may not need you for periods at a time, and if he is your only artist, you will need to have another steady income or be in a shop. Every client is different and piecing together a workload that fits your needs can be challenging but worth it because working in a shop is always a reliable source of clients and income.

Another important reason to try your best to maintain a solid client base in a shop is not only for reliability but also for financial security in case you have significant downtime. Having a plan B when it comes to your financial security is a must. Don't get me wrong; it is possible to work with one private client who stays busy enough for you to be exclusive to only him, but they have to be an A-list star who is protective of their privacy and takes care of their team. I know a barber who is an exclusive barber to a major celebrity and is completely happy with it. His client is a huge A-list celebrity, and he makes great money. This particular artist has a personal entourage of people that have been with him for 20 years, including his barber. He is a very private person, so not too many people come in and out, but he takes care of his team and this barber feels secure enough to know that just being with this one artist works well for him.

On the other hand, I know a barber who had two major artists he was working with and gave up working at the shop to go on tour and cater to them. It was very fun for him, and he was living a great life, until 15 years and two kids of his own down the line, one of his artists wasn't as big anymore and stopped making music and touring, and the other artist just decided one day he wanted to switch barbers, and just like that, my friend never received another call. No explanation or anything, just no more contact with that client. And usually, when an artist does this, you no longer cut the team either. Whoever the new barber is will take over everyone. This was very sad for me to see. He ended up going back into the shop but with no clientele and no investments, nor did he create a company or some type of external income to carry him beyond this business. He did not think of this scenario because he felt as though the artist needed him, so he was completely caught off guard. Essentially, he had to start from scratch. This is very difficult coming from living a certain lifestyle to back in the shop, promoting for new clients and answering everyone's questions. This is why you should always maintain a steady stream of clientele, it's important for you to think ahead for yourself, and your own quality of life.

No matter which of these situations apply to you, you always want to save money and have a plan B. His story kept me grounded and taught me that you have to work smarter and sometimes that means working harder to keep your own business going. Don't take anything for granted, think about YOUR future, and make smart decisions along the way. It's important to have faith, know your self-worth, and work hard, but you also want to start creating and think of what's next for you. Look at the bigger picture and build your future even while you are working hard right now.

Handling the Pressure
Despite the priceless moments and having a dream job, all of this can be very stressful, and you will take a lot of falls along the way. Because of the fast-paced lifestyle, mentally you could go

back and forth with a lot of different issues and be handling multiple things at once. You may not have anyone who really understands what you are going through or be able to offer full support, and that can feel isolating. I work very hard and only really have time for my family. Although they know how crazy my schedule is, I don't think they fully understand how intense my life really is sometimes. You have to be strong-minded and ready for anything. The only thing that relieves me from my stress is to spend my off time with the people I love or doing something I love to do. Learning to appreciate the small things are important and realizing how valuable your time and energy are is priceless.

I will be at the shop during the day saying I'm glad I'm off tomorrow, and the next thing I know, I'm on a last-minute flight to Atlanta that night. Unexpected craziness is the story of my life. I'm sharing so that if this is a dream of yours, you can know exactly what you can expect and how to prepare. If things seem to become overwhelming, remember that the hardest parts of life are when you grow the most!

To stay prepared for any unexpected work nights, always carry your tools with you in case you have to leave at any given moment for work. I recommend having two sets of all of your equipment, so you can leave one at the shop and carry one with you. You always have to stay ready, so I make it a habit to always have my backpack with my clippers everywhere I go.

Also, anytime you are traveling to another state and back in one day, take an overnight bag just in case you have to stay or travel to another location. Have this bag ready and in your car. This can seem extreme but it is best to be prepared. You will find it will make your life easier and you will be able to be more reliable and efficient.

"

*Focus leads to achievement and
achievement leads to success.*

"

Chapter Eleven

The Business Side

Once you cultivate the important rules, develop a strong work ethic, and learn to manage business and personal stresses, you can now put your focus on building your business and professionalism. The goal is to work towards a successful career in the entertainment industry. To help prepare you for the financial side of the business, we will discuss understanding your value, setting your rates, what to expect from being on set, house calls and travel, how to invoice for these jobs, as well as incorporating some of the ins-and-outs of the industry and other opportunities you have available to you that we touched on earlier in Chapter Eight .

This side of the business will involve some ups and downs and trials and errors. This is expected, so don't be too hard on yourself when things get tough. It will take time to get familiar with how things operate in this business, but it is critical to succeeding. Distractions will be all around you, so remain professional, make sure your business is together and organized, be reliable, keep your mind in a business mindset, and stay focused. Focus leads to achievement and achievement leads to success.

Understanding Your Value

The first thing you should know as a barber or hairstylist in the entertainment business is your value is immeasurable, and you are very essential. Whatever photoshoot, video, or event your client has will not happen until they meet with you to be cut, styled, or groomed first. Even if it's just a house call to get freshened up, you make the difference in whether he feels good enough to step out or be photographed. Unfortunately, at times this industry has a way of making you feel last to be recognized for all of your sacrifices. You may often feel your talent and ability are taken for granted, and you may have to stand up for yourself to get all the credit you deserve, therefore, I'm here to let you know, you are amazing at what you do, and you have just as much credibility as the next person. It takes an entire team, including the artist, to make this job successful. So, because you are necessary and will be making a lot of sacrifices to make sure your job is done efficiently and to the best of your ability, you are entitled to charge what you feel your time and talent is worth. Never forget your talent and effort is valuable and so is your time.

Financial Management:

Working in the entertainment industry comes with its own financial management. While there are some similarities to managing your finances working in a barbershop, you have more to consider in the entertainment industry. Here we will discuss setting your rates for house calls, traveling and while you are on set. Also invoicing for these and keeping track of your work.

Setting Rates

Deciding what to charge in this industry can be a hard thing to determine. You will be charging significantly more than you would in the shop; granted, but regardless of the time and effort you made to get there, some clients can feel like you're overcharging them because it's just a haircut and they think your rates are high, and on the contrary, some will feel insulted if you charge too little. This makes it difficult. But, by no means let the fact that this is a fun job, you get to be around amazing people that are otherwise inaccessible, and the fact you get to travel get in the way of what you should be charging. You will need to be available, sometimes at the last minute, from a couple of hours to get your client ready, to an all-day scheduled shoot with long days, to a few days when you are on the road. Plus, there are the typical stresses that also come along with it. Regardless of the fun or the pressures, this is a demanding job; you are a licensed professional, it is a sacrifice, you are very necessary, and you need to be paid. Bottom line is: This your livelihood and it's important that you are compensated for all you do.

You will also be charging differently for house calls, traveling, and set rates. When considering your rates, you will need to factor in location, travel, and time. If you're doing a house call and the client is new and you are unsure, you can always ask them what their normal barber charges and go from there.

I can't tell you what to charge, but for house calls, you can consider what you charge in the shop and add your time and travel. Typically starts at $100, but that's usually for just a beard, and it depends on where (how far) you have to go. You should make it worth your while, but at the same time, keep it within reason. You don't want to overcharge or undervalue your work and get stuck at a low rate. So, you have to charge for your worth and for your time, but be careful of overcharging. I have seen some barbers overcharge because the client is a celebrity and it is assumed they can afford it. This is true, but I believe it is more about the principle. Barbers that have overcharged lose out on a lot of opportunities, especially if they are new to the game and don't have a reputable status. It often takes time to build this up. I feel like you should believe in yourself and charge what you think your talent is worth, but you should also be aware of the risk of overcharging. Sometimes it's not about charging a large fee a few times; it's about longevity and opportunity. A lot of the opportunities you will have will come from your own clients. If you really feel the need to charge an excessive amount and you have a valid reason for your rates, discuss them so you can be on the same page.

When traveling for a client, your rates can vary, but a lot of times these rates can be discussed with the management and an agreement can be made before you travel, depending on how far you have to go and the amount of work that is being done. I have a client that I fly all over for just to do his beard. I feel bad charging him high rates, but there is a risk in traveling and I'm taking most, if not all, of my day to get to him. Yes, it's a beard, and yes, he pays for my flight, driver, and accommodations as well. But, despite the fact it's just a beard, I still have to charge him for all the time and energy it takes for me to get to him; plus, I take into consideration an entire day of no other work getting done. My time is very valuable, and this can be overwhelming at times, especially when it's last minute. I don't charge him as much as I would a client with the same travel, and I have to perform a full retwist and line-up on, but I charge him enough to compensate for the time involved and the travel. So, things like this need to be addressed, stressed and understood on both sides, but ultimately your time, effort, and talent should be compensated.

Regardless, keep your rates consistent for each individual client, although you may be charging differently for each one. Whatever you decided to charge each client, write it down and keep these rates consistent for house calls and regular service travels (meaning, not for shoots with travel –those rates will be more– but this way you will know exactly how to charge and what you're charging for). Honestly, when I first started, I charged each client differently depending on who they were because I had no idea what amount was appropriate, and I'm sure at times I undercharged. Now, I still have different rates depending on the client and what gigs we have but I have put my rates at an amount that I feel my value is compensated and I feel appreciated for my talent.

With set rates, while working with celebrity clients and dealing with record labels or production on big professional sets, just remember to stand up for your rates and your talent. Don't be afraid to discuss rates if you feel you should be paid more. In this industry, you have to say what you want, or you won't get it. As long as you have a valid reason, you will probably get what you ask for. Sometimes production will try to offer you a low amount just to see if you will take it. I find this insulting and I stick to my rates, especially if a video is overnight or a full day. And granted, you have a lot of downtime, but your hours on set add up regardless of the amount of time spent waiting in between takes. When you are asked for your rates, it's always better to come in high so that you can negotiate down. If you work privately for a client and he requests you be there, and production or the label is paying you, you can charge accordingly. Production will pay what they have to because you are the personal barber or hairstylist. They are aware these artists cannot or possibly will not perform or shoot if they do not look the part and feel their best. This is why we are so important. Set your rates to equate this worth.

So remember, Keep track of what you charge

for each client. Although rates vary, keep them consistent for house calls, travel, photoshoots, videos, and anything else they may have. Since your rate will also vary when dealing with production or other companies for jobs your artist may do, find a day rate (a standard rate you will charge for a half-day or full-day), with consideration to the hours involved and travel time to location. These rates will most likely be higher.

Remember, you are charging professional rates so be professional, dependable, on time, prepared, and most of all, irreplaceable.

Invoices

After doing a house call, sometimes the artist will pay you directly, but when you are on set or traveling, you will have to submit an invoice before you can get paid. Sometimes this can take anywhere from a few days to a few weeks, so be prepared to wait. Keep track and pay attention to all your invoices and what money you have floating around, and mark them paid soon as they come in. Usually, when you have been with an artist for a while, you will be put on payroll (this is when you are paid through direct deposit) from his finance people.

However, if production or the label is paying your invoice, it will take longer because along with an invoice, you may have to submit a W-9 and/or bank account information. All production companies handle their payroll differently, some processes are simple; some require more paperwork. Invoices can be kind of difficult at first, but you just have to find a good invoice app that you can use directly from your phone. I like to complete my invoices on the job so I don't forget, and if I need any information, it's available right there. I currently use Invoice2go; PayPal has one as well. But you can choose one that has high ratings and go from there. Once you get used to it, it's pretty easy.

On the Go

Being on the go can add a whole new busyness to your life. You will have to be prepared for long busy days on set, to last-minute house calls and unexpected travel. It sounds exciting, but it is a lot of work. There is a lot of responsibility to endure on these jobs, and the pressure can sometimes be intimidating, but with a little preparedness, you can be ready for anything! Let's discuss what life on set, doing house calls, and traveling entails and how to make it go as smoothly as possible.

Life on Set

From the very beginning, my experience on set has been an interesting challenge; figuring out everything as I went. For instance, when we were doing videos, production typically hires someone for hair and makeup for everybody including the artist. But I would show up for my artist and often people would look confused and would ask my client, "You brought your own barber?" As this was becoming the new normal, they had to be made aware that he was bringing his own barber, and when we received the call sheet before each video, it would say "Hair" or "Barber" next to my name. After some time, I started making sure his face and hair were looking fresh, and I incorporated things he needed like lotions, lip balm, powder, etc. This has not only changed my title on set, it has also made me more valuable, more in demand, and has brought in more income for me. It definitely set me apart from everyone else. I realized I needed a title that better conveyed my role, so I decided I would refer to myself as the Groomer and be specific about what I offered. It stuck and now that is the title. This was an interesting process for me. There aren't too many barbers that are groomers, so you will definitely be an asset if you can offer this service.

When you are at events such as videos, commercials, editorials, award shows, red carpet, etc. You have to come prepared. Be sure to always arrive on set an hour before your client so you have time for any delays, like finding parking or having to shuttle to the location. You should always be set up and ready by the time your client arrives. It is unprofessional if you show up at the same time or late. Any time they will be on camera for an extended amount of time, you will have to be ready to groom them. This means making sure they look camera-ready in between wardrobe changes and scenes. Make sure you have everything your client likes such as a particular lip balm, lotion, hair products, etc. and have it easily accessible.

I like to have a list of things that each client prefers so I can have anything they might need set up for them when they arrive. This shows that you are professional, and you care about their needs. Make sure you have a set bag to carry with you to keep all your necessities in. This is a bag that you will have everything you use for that client, that you will pre-pack and carry with you at all times while you are on set. Be sure to consider the weather if you are shooting outside. Your bag will typically include brush or comb, lip balm, small lotion, powder, powder brush, hand sanitizer, oil blotting sheets, paper towels, hand wipes, and anything else you use often for your client. They are all different and they all like certain brands. Make your bag customizable to that client.

If a new job is being offered to you, then be competitive with your prices because they may go with someone else. If you are doing full grooming, you can charge double what you would to just cut them but take into consideration how many hours the set will run, or you could always charge a day rate. If someone questions your price, be ready to tell them all that is included and focus on the value you provide to the client. It always has to make sense; you will sometimes have to turn down work if someone isn't willing to pay enough to make it worth your time.

You will eventually not be questioned about the amount you charge if you build a reputable status. This will take years of hard consistent work and building solid relationships, but it is worth it, and it will keep you busy.

Part of being successful in this industry not only requires being professional but it also means you need to be on top of your creative skills, performing your best possible work, and being able to bring visions to reality. There will be treatments available for you to look at, this is basically a pictured story giving you the details of the shoot, including looks and visuals. However, you never know what will be required on set or which creative direction an artist will go, so you have to be ready to adapt to changing trends and visions that are hard to achieve. This is when your creativity and skill come into play. I suggest you educate yourself and take classes or workshops whenever possible to enhance your arsenal of talents.

There is a printable version of set etiquette and what to include in your set bag available on my website at www.TheHairMint.com.

House Calls and Travel

House calls are a service that you will provide to your exclusive clientele who are most likely too popular or too busy to go to a shop. They will pay more for you to come to them. House calls are not easy because you are traveling to a location, finding somewhere to set up and take out your equipment, cleaning everything after, packing up, and going to your next location. You are not in your typical setting with good lighting and a mirror. This is where your practice comes in and developing "Barber's Eye" becomes necessary. Barber's eye is talent you develop over time where you are able to see your weight or heaviness in your haircut without looking in the mirror. This takes some practice but is very important if you plan on doing house calls or traveling to locations for your clients other than the shop. To practice the Barber's eye, once you have finished your haircut, look in the mirror to see your weight lines (areas that are heavy or need to be blended) then look back at your haircut and find the weight line you saw in the mirror. Next try and see your weight lines without the mirror and then check to see if your right. Keep practicing you will eventually be able to see it without the help of the mirror. This will save you a lot of time, plus once you have finished your client and they have gotten up, they may not want to sit back down to fix anything you might see. So, make sure you are consistent and efficient with your haircuts.

You are also setting your equipment up on a chair, table, dresser, couch, pretty much anywhere you can. You are always making adjustments, so because of these unorthodox settings, you will most likely take longer to complete your haircuts. Aside from all of your tools and products, always remember to bring a headlamp or a ring light; I prefer a headlamp, so you can see pretty well under any circumstances and an extension cord in case you are far from an outlet.

Traveling can be time-consuming as well, depending on where you're going and if you are staying overnight. When you travel, I would charge a day rate according to your overall time commitment. I live in California and if I have to fly to Las Vegas, I can go cut my client and come right back and it will take a half-day. But if I have to fly to Atlanta or New York and come right back, it will take the entire day. Charge accordingly. Usually, all of your expenses are covered, and you can be reimbursed if you have to pay for anything like an Uber or airport parking. Most of the time you will have a driver at the airport waiting to pick you up to take you to your hotel or directly to the artist, the discretion is up to your client. Usually, you will work all the details out with management. When you travel, make sure you pack as light as possible and try not to check a bag, as bags can get lost and sometimes you won't have time to go to baggage claim.

When traveling by air, packing your clippers are fine but do not take any shears over five inches, and do not carry a full pack of new blades, as a matter of fact do not carry any, if they find them they will make you throw them away, check your bag or confiscate them. This will be an unnecessary delay or a problem, and also make sure you have don't have a blade inside your razor. If need be, you can ask management if they can have blades for you when you arrive or allow time for you to go get them. If you don't follow TSA regulations and they find your razor with a blade in it, they will throw your entire razor away! Also, follow TSA rules for approved liquids, and don't forget to bring your headlamp and extension cord. Take a picture of the terminal you parked in, leave a parking ticket inside your car, keep all of your receipts, and have a safe and productive trip!!

Regardless if you are doing house calls or traveling on the road once you arrive your attention and priority is on your client. Your time revolves around your client, and it is important that you make sure he is taken care of first before you tend to anything else.

Industry Options

As we discussed earlier in Chapter eight there are quite a few industry options you have to choose from. They are all exciting careers and the great thing is, you don't have to choose just one. Once you are in the industry you will have tons of opportunities and room to grow and explore. You can choose to make your own decisions and control your own path by building you own clientele, or instead of controlling every aspect of your career, there are other directions you can go that can be a great change. Attaining an agent is one of them, they will pick up a lot of the responsibility you would normally carry being your own boss. Another option is the TV and Film industry, which is the goal for a lot of creative barbers and stylists who want to see their work on the big screen. Both of these options may spark a new creative fire for you. Let's discuss this more in detail here.

Work for Yourself or Get an Agent
You can take a lot of routes in this industry. You

can be like me and work independently with high-profile clients, where you do your own networking, negotiations, and handle your own schedule, invoices, and charge your own prices. Or you could work for an independent agent or one who works for a top agency that has the access to get you gigs, doing major commercials, A-list photoshoots, editorials, etc. Major companies often like to reach out to agencies they are familiar with to send them hair and makeup people because they are not so worried about paying more than they are for looking more for someone who has the credentials to do the job they are expecting, understands the rules, and is professional. As we discussed earlier, along with sealing the deal for you, agents also handle your rates, make sure you are treated well on set, handle any problems, and submit invoices for payment. They try and get you the highest paid jobs because they do get a percentage, and these jobs are usually really reputable and are hard to get on your own.

An agent also has full control of your schedule, although they discuss it with you, they are in control of all of your jobs. So any clients you currently work with are booked through them and they get a percentage of it all. They will negotiate all your rates, getting you paid top dollar, whether you had been working with a client previously or not, and they are also more likely to start charging your personal clients more as well, so you would have to take that risk and if you plan on working in a shop, depending how busy your agent keeps you, make sure you stay ahead of your schedule as much as possible so you can book your clients accordingly.

For me, it's quite the change; having an agent doesn't work for me because I have too many clients, and the change will interrupt my schedule too much. But if this is something you want to look into, keep working on your versatility, start taking pictures and put together an online portfolio, and keep track of the opportunities you are getting outside the shop because you have to show experience to be picked up by an agency. If this is what you are interested in, go for it!

The Union
There is another side to this industry, and that is the union (in my area and craft, it's the 706 Union supported by IATSE). This is the union where your jobs will be on longer sets for film and television, or anything mandatory to be covered by the union. These jobs usually go on for a duration of time, depending on how long the project is and can be almost like a job where you are scheduled to be there for a certain amount of time each day and can even require relocating. The union protects you from different issues and provides paid overtime, holiday pay, essential rest, and pretty much just makes sure you are treated right according to their different provisions. The union also offers great medical and pension benefits. However, it is not simple to join. You can join in a few ways.

One way is the 60–60–60. You have to complete 60 days of non-roster work experience in each of three years of work, within the last five-year period, in Los Angeles County on sets such as network television, videos, or non-union film or television production. If you want to go this route, it is important to know that when you join the union, you either qualify under hair or makeup. At the moment they don't have barbering, so if you are a barber, you will qualify under makeup to do men's grooming. If you have your cosmetologist license, you qualify under hair and you can do women's and men's grooming. Earlier we discussed having dual licenses (both barber and cosmologist); this would be a perfect example of the opportunity you will have.

If you're only doing or just starting to do music videos and eventually want to apply for the union, make sure your name is on all the call sheets for the video you are doing under hair or grooming so you can get the credit and get it counted toward your days because you have to show proof of work. You can also apply for the union if you have worked on one set for 30 consecutive days. Not 28 or 29, it has to be 30 or it won't count. Or if the main actor who is scheduled to be in the movie requests you to be on set with him, you can then be allowed to work and then apply to be in the union if you choose, after. But you have to show proof that you have worked with this actor or artist previously on set for some time for this to be approved. You also have to pay your initiation dues to join. This is a one-time payment. It's a bit pricy, $6,000 for makeup, and $5,500 for hair. They require half down and the other half to be paid in six months. After initiation, the dues to remain working are $262.97 and must be paid quarterly on or before January 1st, April 1st, July 1st, and October 1st. Any member who accepts work and is behind in their payments is subject to fines. This is a responsibility, but the money you make and the benefits you get make it worth it. You are not required to take every job that comes up, but they make sure you get offered enough so you can afford to pay your dues. A lot of people like the movie and television industry because of the stability and the benefits, which as you know as barbers and hairdressers we don't get on our own, but it can be like any job, long hours with the same people until that job is over.

These are all exciting avenues you can aspire to take on, just remember to move with purpose and prepare yourself throughout your journey. I wish you much success in all of your creative and career endeavors.

From the Heart

At this point in my life, I have been on the go for the last 10 years in an the entertainment industry, and I have to say I have accomplished more in these last 10 years than I ever have in my entire life. It's been a wild journey and I have learned valuable lessons along the way. I am forever grateful for my talent but more so for my perseverance, strength, guidance, and the protection I have received along the way.

I have realized that my ultimate goal is to contribute to something beyond myself and to inspire barbers and hairstylists to do whatever it is they want to do within the extraordinary hair industry, and to encourage them to keep working hard and follow their dreams even when the journey gets difficult.

I hope that through reading this book, you have learned that no matter what happens, where you go, or how many shops you decide to work in, nobody can take away anything you have acquired along the way. And anywhere you go, your expertise and experience will always go with you. This is where taking the time to invest in yourself becomes so priceless. I know this industry can be a lot to take in and consider; but it's also a rewarding challenge, and I know it is a passion for some of you. I sincerely hope every chapter has helped to give you some insight, knowledge and encouragement to become a better you.

I hope you realize all of your setbacks are inside

of you, and it's up to you to push through for a higher success. Even if the dream seems like it's just a dream, believe in yourself, be persistent, stay focused and keep going. You will receive everything you are asking for; it is how the universe works. Be patient and don't worry about how, just be ready for when. There is always a new chapter in life; don't be afraid to start it!

This is my new chapter, and I hope it helps you find inspiration, motivation, and passion for your purpose so you can also inspire others, and we can make this world a better place. We all have a purpose in life; it's up to us to find it, live it, and share it —Be Legendary.

Tracy Love

Be Legendary

PLEASE USE THE FOLLOWING PAGES TO WRITE DOWN ANY GOALS OR IDEAS YOU MAY HAVE AND TAKE NOTES!

ALSO FEEL FREE TO GO TO MY WEBSITE:
THEHAIRMINT.COM

* *TO CHECK OUT MY PORTFOLIO AND SOME OF MY WORK*
* *TO DOWNLOAD A PRINTABLE LIST OF THE SHOP QUESTION (CHAPTER 6)*
* *DOWNLOAD A PRINTABLE LIST OF YOUR MALE GROOMING SETLIST (CHAPTER 11)*
* *TO PURCHASE MERCHANDISE*

AND

* *TO SIGN UP FOR EMAIL UPDATES ON ANY FUTURE RELEASES OR UPCOMING BOOK TOUR DATES!*

Goals

_____

_____

_____

_____

_____

_____

_____

_____

_____

_____

_____

_____

_____

Goals

_____

_____

_____

_____

_____

_____

_____

_____

_____

_____

_____

_____

_____

_____

Ideas

Ideas

Notes

Notes

_____

_____

_____

_____

_____

_____

_____

_____

_____

_____

_____

_____

_____

_____

Notes

Notes

_____

_____

_____

_____

_____

_____

_____

_____

_____

_____

_____

_____

_____

_____

_____

Aknowledgments

First and foremost, I would like to thank you God for always protecting me and my family and being there when I needed to talk. Thank you for giving me everything I asked for when you knew I was ready to receive it. I would not be who I am without you. I am grateful and forever thankful.

I would like to thank my family for being the backbone of my success:

Sherah~ Thank you for being the big sister and holding the house together through all the late nights and traveling, my journey would not of been possible without you and I appreciate you for all you have done, thank you for being the supportive, encouraging, and loving person you are.

Kaaria~ thank you for being the sweet, smart and talented young lady you have grown into, thank you for your support all these years. Thank you for being the photographer in the family and taking the picture for the cover of this book, it means the world.

Tory~ Thank you for your support as well son, and for not driving everyone crazy. You are a super special talented young man with a lot of drive and passion for what you do. Thank you for the music for the trailer for this book it means so much. I am super proud and excited for you and I can't wait to hear how you change the world.

Jaedyn, Ryan and Riley you guys are something else, but I am proud of you guys and I love you with all my heart!! You all have been there every single day supporting me throughout my journey and I appreciate you guys for making all the sacrifices you have for me. I love you all forever.

Mom~ Thank you for all the conversations on my long drive home and being there for me when I felt no one would understand. I want to thank you for all your sacrafices you have made for me and everything you have done for me throughout my life. I get my hard work, independent, conscientious mindset from you, and I am thankful for you making me into who I am. I love you!

Kobe Bryant~ Thank you for being the inspiration behind the title of this book, you will always be the greatest and forever missed. We love you.

Nipsey Hussle~ Thank you forever for helping me continue my purpose and inspiring me to write this book, you have changed my life.

Wiz~ It's been almost a decade together and I want to thank you for always believing in me and trusting me. I sincerely appreciate you for taking me everywhere with you, thank you for all of the amazing experiences You are forever family to me. Thank you for being one of my biggest inspirations. I love you.

To my Chops family~ Cynthia you are the best boss, thank you for being who you are, we need more people like you in this world. I appreciate you for letting me use the barbershop picture for the back of this book, it really means a lot! And to all the barbers Josh, Zay, Joe, and Lisa thank you guys for being such good friends and supporting me throughout my writing process and my crazy life. We have been through a lot together and we always stick together that's why I love being there. I honestly don't think there's another shop like us. I love you guys.

Joy~ We have been friends for 15 years and have been through a lot, thank you for all the laughs, good times and always being my extended family.

To my clients~ I am grateful for you all, thank you for all the great conversations, laughs, and allowing me into your lives. Some of you have been there from the beginning and I appreciate you for all your patience and dedication throughout the years. Thank you for believing in me and trusting me when your hair.

Biography

Tracy Love is licensed in both Cosmetology and Barbering and has specialized in men's haircare for almost 20 years. She has moved throughout her career with the intention to master haircutting and perfect her craft.

She has done Hair Shows up and down the Westcoast, including Las Vegas and Arizona doing platform work and private educational classes for one of the biggest clipper companies in the world, Andis, for 6 years.

This has set her up to make her mark in the Entertainment Industry for the last 10 years and counting. She has worked with and continues to be the personal Barber/Groomer to some of the biggest Music Artists in the world including Wiz Khalifa, Big Sean, 2Chainz, Travis Scott, Juicy J, Russ, Chris Brown, Ty Dolla$ign, Swae Lee, Mike Posner, and more! She has also worked with TV greats such as O'Shea Jackson Jr., Ice Cube, Ice T, Billy Dee Williams and more!

Together with her clients she has done many Talk Shows such as Ellen, Jimmy Kimmel, The Tonight Show, Good Morning America, Ridiculousness, Revolt TV, The Real, The New Arsenal Hall Show, and His and Hers on ESPN. Along with Red Carpets for A-listed Filmed Events for TV. She has done tons of Music Videos and Editorials for just about every Entertainment and Fashion Magazine including the Double Cover Power 30 Issue of Source Magazine, Vogue Italy and Playboy. She has also done many Commercials including three Super Bowl Commercials for Pepsi, T-Mobile, and Expensify. She has also done Commercials for Oreo, Adidas, Reebok, Google Pixel, Gatorade, Beats by Dre and more. She has also groomed her clients for Red Carpets and performances for Award Shows including the Grammy's, BET Awards, MTV Video Music Awards, BillBoard Music Awards and iHeart Radio.

She continues to travel across the United States doing what she has so much passion for and working for people she is inspired by. Above all her successes this book is by far the most challenging yet rewarding achievement she has accomplished.

And although her life is priceless and her time is of most value, there is no where she would rather be than at home with her family, who are the heartbeat for all of her hard work.

Check out my Portfolio on TheHairMint.com! By Tracy Love.

Thank you for purchasing this book! I'm looking forward to doing more exciting things! Hopefully I will see you at upcoming shows and events to answer any questions you may have about this book!!

Please check my website for updates!!

Feel free to reach out to me!

Website: TheHairMint.com
Facebook: www. Facebook.com/TheHairMint
Instagram: tlovecutz

CPSIA information can be obtained
at www.ICGtesting.com
Printed in the USA
LVHW082039101021
700094LV00001B/1